AMEN CORNER

AMEN CORNER

How the National Media Shaped Public Opinion on Gay Marriage

Gwen Richardson

AMEN CORNER. Copyright © 2013 by Gwen Richardson. All rights reserved. Printed in the United States of America. No part of this book may be used or reproduced in any manner whatsoever without written permission except in the case of brief quotations embodied in critical articles and reviews. For information, contact Cushcity Communications, 14300 Cornerstone Village Dr., Suite 370, Houston, TX 77014.

FIRST EDITION

Cover design by Rosamond Grupp

ISBN: 9780980025002
ISBN-10: 0980025001

10 9 8 7 6 5 4 3 2 1

Printed in the United States of America

*To all those who have been and will be
persecuted for supporting traditional marriage*

TABLE OF CONTENTS

INTRODUCTION 1

CHAPTER 1: Hijacking the Civil Rights Movement 11

CHAPTER 2: Stacking the Deck 36

CHAPTER 3: Carrots and Sticks 49

CHAPTER 4: Sticks and Stones May Break My Bones. 59

CHAPTER 5: Prevarication and Mendacity 67

CHAPTER 6: Endorsing the "Born That Way" Myth 94

CHAPTER 7: Endorsing the "If You're Gay, You Can't Change" Myth 111

CHAPTER 8: Everything's Coming Up Roses 125

CHAPTER 9: See No Evil, Hear No Evil 151

CHAPTER 10: Sins of Omission 162

CHAPTER 11: Playing the Numbers Game 173

CHAPTER 12: We Only Report Poll Results That We Like. 178

CHAPTER 13: Help From Hollywood 185

CHAPTER 14: What Should the American Public Do? 194

CHAPTER 15: What Comes Next? 198

INTRODUCTION

In 2004, Gallup polls showed that 42 percent of Americans supported gay marriage. Eight years later, by the end of 2012, support had jumped to 53 percent.[1] Public opinion seemed to change at a rapid pace, almost overnight. How did it shift so quickly? The answer is: the media.

In the same way that a small cadre of enthusiastic supporters in the amen corner of a church agrees with the preacher's every utterance from the pulpit, the media have been consistent champions for gay marriage and lesbian-gay-bisexual-transgender (LGBT) causes. If there were any doubts about the opinions of media representatives regarding gay marriage, all doubts were removed on June 26, 2013 when the Supreme Court struck down the Defense of Marriage Act (DOMA). The celebratory mood in some newsrooms was palpable. The only things missing were the sounds of champagne corks popping and the visual of a confetti drop.

The national media would have the public believe that opinion polls shifted based solely on an organic evolution of attitudes. In fact, considering the way media have enthusiastically championed gay marriage, the news is not that public opinion has shifted, but that, in spite of the one-sided media coverage, nearly half the country still opposes it. And because, as a result of syndication and wire services, the national media strongly influence what is reported locally, the nature of their coverage is all the more important.

The shift in opinion did not occur among those who had already made up their minds. For those who are solidly liberal and support gay marriage, media coverage probably helped them bolster their position. For those who are solidly conservative, media coverage did not dissuade them and their opposition was likely reinforced. But for those in the middle who had not made up their minds one way or the other, the biased media coverage did have a persuasive impact.

Moreover, the additional boost in the polling may very well be, in part, the result of the fear of browbeating and intimidation directed toward survey respondents. It is entirely feasible that 10 percent (or about 5 percentage points) of the people who respond to surveys in support of gay marriage are doing so because they do not want to be verbally attacked, perceived as "bigots," or experience retaliation for being in opposition. They have seen how the media treat those who disagree – and it's not pretty.

A Pew Research Center poll released in June 2013 confirms the media's bias. The Center studied news coverage during the period marked by Supreme Court deliberations on the subject of gay marriage, from March 18 to May 12, and found the news stories supporting same-sex marriage outnumbered those opposing it by roughly 5 to 1.[2] In actuality, the bias is even more pronounced than this study demonstrates, particularly for television, because the predisposition of the moderator, news anchor and producer are not taken into account. In the vast majority of on-air discussions about same-sex marriage, the moderator's bias in favor of gay marriage is apparent. This lack of neutrality further skews the overall coverage.

Without the media as such an omnipresent and aggressive ally, it is doubtful that the issue of gay marriage would have gained the level of traction it has experienced over the past two decades. By the very nature of their profession, journalists are supposed to be impartial arbiters of the truth and present the public with as even-handed and unbiased a portrayal of the facts as possible. They are not supposed to be advocates for a particular social policy. But rather than carry out their journalistic charge to fairly present both sides of this issue and let the public decide, the mainstream media have abdicated their role as objective observers and, instead, have been cheerleaders for the cause. And they have been doing so for at least 20 years.

On Dec. 28, 1992, CNN aired a report regarding children who were raised by lesbians. The report cited a study conducted by Charlotte Patterson, a psychologist who was, coincidentally, a lesbian herself. The study measured the social adjustment of children living in San Francisco-area households headed by lesbians. Thirty-seven households participated in the study, and the children's ages ranged from the kindergarten to elementary school levels.

Patterson's study concluded that not only were children from such households well-adjusted, in some cases they were "better-adjusted" than children from traditional families. The CNN announcer, in a voice-over, used the descriptive terms, "perfectly normal," "high self-esteem," and "more happiness" to describe children raised in these homes. The announcer also indicated lesbian women gave birth to about 5,000 children each year.

Clearly, there were several flaws in this type of reporting which CNN failed to point out. First, a study with such a small sample size is not scientific and, therefore, not credible based on accepted research standards. Second, because the researcher was herself a lesbian and, therefore, had a stake in the study's outcome, there was a built-in bias. Third, pre-pubescent children are not yet at a point in their lives where the long-term effects of these living arrangements can be accurately assessed. It is likely that, at a minimum, their views on family structures would be significantly different than those of children raised in nuclear families.

Fourth, since homosexuals, by definition, are supposedly not sexually attracted to the opposite sex, how are the children produced? Were the lesbians once married to males whom they later abandoned to form relationships with their female partners, bringing the children along with them? The network's report was silent on these matters.

Finally, stating that these children are "better adjusted" than those from traditional households makes an inappropriate and unsubstantiated value judgment; in other words, the researcher concluded that this lifestyle produces results which are *superior* to those of the nuclear family. This conclusion strains credulity, since nearly every study conducted on child development has shown that the ideal arrangement which consistently produces the best results is a household where a child's biological parents (male/female) are married and living under the same roof.

Print media joined forces with television news networks to promote gay marriage in the 1990s. The June 21, 1993 issue of *Newsweek*, for example, included a cover story titled, "Lesbians: Coming Out Strong/What Are the Limits of Intolerance?"[3] Pictured on the cover of the magazine and throughout the article were lesbians embracing each other and surrounded by groups of children. The implicit inference in the title was clear: If you disagree with or do not support this lifestyle, you are, therefore, "intolerant."

Fast forward to April 12, 2013 when *Time* magazine released an edition with the cover story, "Gay Marriage Already Won: The Supreme Court Hasn't Made Up Its Mind—But America Has." Inherent in the subtitle is the idea that the entire country approves of gay marriage, when the average polls are at about 50 percent support, depending upon the wording of the questions asked. *Time* published the edition with two cover images -- one with two gay males kissing and the other with two lesbian females kissing.

The concept of a *Time* magazine cover showing any two individuals posing with their lips locked seemed odd to me and I could not remember seeing another one. Usually, *Time's* covers feature a single individual or a conceptual graphic design. I conducted some research and could find only one other *Time* magazine cover that showed a couple kissing and it was the cover which featured the royal wedding of Kate Middleton and Prince William in 2011.

Clearly, *Time*'s cover was an in-your-face move targeting whatever remains of the magazine's readership that still believes in traditional marriage between a man and a woman. Rather than reporting the issue of gay marriage with objectivity, "*Time* magazine went all-in on gay marriage," as the Huffington Post described it.[4] Coincidentally, the editor-in-chief of *Time*, Martha Nelson, is gay, according to *Out* magazine.[5]

Through a carefully orchestrated system of selective reporting, slanted coverage and rewards and punishments, national media like CNN, *Newsweek, Time* and others have gradually nudged public opinion in the direction of approval of gay marriage. In recent years, media's coverage has become increasingly one-sided to the point where it is now rare that someone opposing gay marriage will even be interviewed on news broadcasts.

If an individual in opposition to gay marriage is invited as a guest on a news program, the typical scenario is that the person is vilified by the host in the lead-in before the commercial break, or when the first question is asked. The proponent of traditional marriage is then asked a series of loaded questions and kept on the defensive until the interview finally ends and the media's message becomes crystal clear: Anyone opposing gay marriage will be branded as an extremist, a bigot, a dinosaur, filled with hate and obviously out of step with the rest of the country.

A typical exchange is the one between MSNBC's news anchor Thomas Roberts in an interview with Maggie Gallagher, founder of the National Organization for Marriage (NOM) on April 2, 2012. According to its website, NOM was founded in

2007 and is a nonprofit organization with a mission to protect traditional marriage and the faith communities that sustain it.

Roberts, who is gay, has a one-hour news slot on weekdays from 11 a.m. to noon EST. He interviewed Gallagher regarding the leaking of an internal NOM document that revealed the organization's work with black and Hispanic pastors who oppose gay marriage. Roberts' first question to Gallagher was: "Maggie, do you defend your own race-baiting to further bigotry and homophobia on a national level?" The question was rude, obviously biased, immediately put Gallagher on the defensive and was unprofessional for anyone who claims to be a "journalist." But it is hardly atypical for those in media who are on a mission to portray anyone who opposes gay marriage as a bigot and a homophobe.

Even worse, in the media's new phraseology, people who believe marriage is between a man and a woman are on the "wrong side of history." Yet, history can only be examined through the prism of hindsight, after years pass and the effects of social or political change become apparent. In other words, whether one is on the right side or the wrong side of history cannot be predicted in advance.

Why is the media's role important? When the entity purporting to be an independent arbiter is so obviously biased, the public receives incomplete or even false information about a particular issue.

A good example occurred during the discussions leading up to the war with Iraq. For weeks leading up to Congress' vote to declare war, media interviewed dozens of individuals, the vast majority of whom were beating the drums for war and presenting worst case scenarios of America waking up to a "mushroom cloud" from an imminent Iraqi nuclear attack. Media would occasionally include individuals who were opposed to the war, but the numbers of those in favor were so overwhelming that, in a matter of weeks, public opinion shifted from opposition to support.

Years later, the public learned that all of the so-called "experts" on the threat Iraq posed to America because of weapons of mass destruction were wrong. The United States went to war under false pretenses. In essence, our government, aided by the media's complicity, was on the wrong side of history. And the shadow of that ill-fated decision will hang over Congress when the legislators make future decisions about potential military engagements.

If the media had presented both sides of the argument in a balanced way, it is unlikely that we would have ever gone to war with Iraq in the first place. Although they have yet to admit their involvement, the media played a key role in the politicians' decision to send troops to Iraq and engage in a conflict which resulted in the deaths of more than 4,000 American soldiers and cost the U.S. treasury more than $1 trillion.[6]

To be sure, there are many newspapers in smaller media markets that still give an even-handed presentation about the issues surrounding gay marriage. But the major newspapers and magazines that have the largest circulations, along with the network and cable television news programs, long ago shed any semblance of objectivity. These publications and channels tout themselves as balanced and objective, not as mouthpieces for liberal political views. They are known as the "mainstream media" because they are supposed to reflect the broad spectrum of American opinion, not tack dramatically to one side or the other.

Fox News is an exception and is known as the voice of the conservative portion of the electorate. As a result, its coverage generally reflects a position on gay marriage that is to the right of the political center. Fox makes no apologies for being conservative, nor does it mask its political persuasion in any way. But even with Fox's conservative slant, the aforementioned Pew Research Center study showed that, during the two months media coverage was examined, the network's stories on gay marriage were 63 percent mixed, 29 percent supportive and 4 percent in opposition.[7]

The national media have been enthusiastic advocates in the promotion of gay marriage and have been methodical in purging or blocking dissenting opinions from being exposed in the public realm. The reasons for this stance are unclear. Perhaps it is related to the strong influence of gay individuals within their ranks, as will be explained within the chapters of this book. Or perhaps it is due to the collective media's unwritten, but strictly enforced, rule that all cultural and social mores that are secular in nature are acceptable, but any beliefs or attitudes that have a religious foundation are outdated and, thus, off limits.

Whatever the reason, the public has a right to know that it is receiving incomplete and, in many cases, inaccurate information regarding the issue of gay marriage. With that knowledge, they can make informed decisions, no matter which conclusions they reach.

Although some may perceive this book as an attack on gay marriage, that is not its primary goal. The central purpose of this book is to place a spotlight on the role the media play in influencing public opinion, not only about gay marriage, but on other issues as well. Its goal is also to increase awareness about the media's powers of persuasion so consumers can begin to examine media coverage with a more critical eye.

CHAPTER 1
HIJACKING THE CIVIL RIGHTS MOVEMENT

Imagine watching a news broadcast in which a political activist describes the murder of a dozen of his compatriots and compares it to the Jewish Holocaust which took place in Europe in the 1940s. The Jewish community would swiftly respond – and rightly so – that while they were sympathetic to the gentleman's plight, a dozen deaths are no comparison to the estimated 6 million Jews slaughtered during World War II.

Yet, for the past 20 years, gay activists have used the 350-year history of African-American slavery, murder, Jim Crow and second-class citizenship – the equivalent of a centuries-long American holocaust – as a stepping stone. An estimated 15 to 35 million blacks were captured in Africa and made the horrific, inhumane, three-month voyage across the Atlantic Ocean.[8] An estimated 25 percent, or 4 to 7 million Africans, perished en route to various ports.[9]

Rather than treat this grisly era and the descendants of those who endured it with the respect and deference they deserve, many gay activists, instead, view it as a mere opportunity; a chance to compare it with the shame, intimidation and humiliation some of them may have encountered due to their same-sex attractions. Sadly, however, there has been no similar outcry, either from black elected officials or members of the media, denouncing this absurd and insulting comparison.

Gay activists made the decision early on to use the Civil Rights Movement as the basis for their argument to legalize gay marriage, but the media's help is what made it possible for this inane comparison to gain traction. Nearly every historical example used by gay activists to demonstrate why gay marriage should be legalized is based upon African-American oppression. They are the only group that fights for rights using not their own history of discrimination, but that of a third party. One wonders what arguments gay activists would use if the African-American legacy was not at their disposal. In essence, they have spent their entire campaign for gay marriage hiding behind their fellow black citizens.

The comparisons would be laughable if their promotion had not achieved a high degree of success. Yet, liberals, moderates and the vast majority of media representatives have bought into the idea that taking a moral position regarding homosexuality is tantamount to discrimination and equivalent to the centuries-long African-American freedom struggle.

Use of Language

The initial strategy used by gay activists was to adopt the language associated with the history of black oppression. Thus, the terms "civil rights," "separate but equal" and "equality" were used as descriptive terms for the gay movement, and the terms "bigot" and "intolerant" were used to describe those in opposition.

Specifically, as it relates to the use of the term "separate but equal," gay individuals have never had to live and operate under any separate-but-equal statutes, as they have always been integrated throughout U.S. society, even while in the closet. In fact, it has been suggested by some that, because they were integrated within American society, they probably owned slaves during the centuries when slavery was legal.

In an address at Harvard Law School in 2004, the Rev. Jesse Jackson made this statement regarding the comparison: "The comparison with slavery is a stretch in that some slave masters were gay, in that gays were never called three-fifths human in the Constitution and in that they did not require the Voting Rights Act to have the right to vote."[10] (Jackson has since changed his position and is now in favor of gay marriage.)

But African Americans languished under these separate but equal -- Jim Crow -- laws for nearly 100 years after slavery ended. After the Civil War and slave emancipation, white Southerners were angry about blacks' newfound freedom and instituted Jim Crow laws to keep blacks in their place. In the late 1890s, "colored" and "white" signs for public restrooms, drinking fountains and train transportation became the law of the land throughout the South. Of course, the colored facilities were always substandard compared to those for whites. These signs remained all over the South until the mid-1960s with the advent of the federal Civil Rights Act and the Public Accommodations Bill.

In Hollywood, when gay actors like Rock Hudson and Montgomery Clift were paid top dollar and given leading movie roles while keeping their lifestyle in the closet, black actors were experiencing the movie industry's version of separate but equal. During the filming of "Gone With the Wind," black actor Lennie Bluett, working as an extra, said he was so shocked to see signs for lavatories that were marked "colored" and "white" that he and other black actors protested. Their efforts went nowhere until Bluett approached Clark Gable, whom Bluett said was outraged by this treatment of the colored performers. Once Gable voiced his anger, the signs, said Bluett, were removed.[11]

Media Joined In With Comparisons

Early on, members of the media joined liberals and gay activists in comparing black civil rights with those of homosexuals. Examples of this comparison in news coverage are numerous, but here are two recent ones.

During a discussion on gay marriage on NBC's March 31, 2013 broadcast of "Meet the Press," substitute host Chuck Todd highlighted a poll from 1968 which showed public opinion on interracial marriage. The poll asked the question: Do you approve of marriage between whites and non-whites? Just 20 percent approved and, as Todd said, "[the Supreme Court] got rid of those laws that they said discriminated." Clearly, Todd considered interracial marriage and gay marriage as equivalent.

On CNN's "Piers Morgan" show on April 3, 2013, Morgan interviewed radio talk show host Michael Reagan, son of President Ronald Reagan, whose news column published that day had mentioned that churches should take a stand against same sex marriage. Morgan challenged Reagan by saying, "There were people throughout America in the 1950s and 1960s who said, 'I know a few black people, but I don't want them to marry my girl.'"

It appears that in the minds of media representatives, the issues of gay marriage and interracial marriage are one and the same, even though the latter was always between a man and a woman. And they continue to draw other parallels where none exist.

Rachel Maddow of MSNBC subtly hinted that discrimination against gay individuals could exist in the same form that it had against blacks for decades. "If you live in one of the 29 states that do not have employment anti-discrimination laws based on sexual orientation," Maddow said during her May 7, 2013 program, "there's nothing in state law that stops a business from putting up a sign that says, 'gays need not apply.'" In actuality, there have never been signs of this nature posted barring homosexuals from access to businesses or employment. But blacks lived under this code of signs for at least 100 years.

Maddow goes on to assert that a person can be fired if they are gay or their boss thinks they are gay. Is she arguing that a gay person cannot be fired for cause? What if the person is incompetent, insubordinate or repeatedly fails to show up for work? Is he or she shielded from being fired because they are gay and the employer could, therefore, be sued? More importantly, how will the employer automatically know that the individual is gay? The question certainly cannot be included on employment applications.

And what occurs in cases where a gay individual is sexually harassing a fellow employee or subordinate? Is he or she immune from legal action simply because of their sexual orientation? What happens to the rights of the heterosexual workers? Are homosexuals considered to be victims in every conceivable situation, even when the facts reveal otherwise? These are all questions that have yet to be addressed in the current political environment.

Moreover, if Maddow and other gay activists have their way, people who publicly oppose gay marriage will soon be at risk of being fired in all 50 states. An ordinance which was enacted on Sept. 5, 2013 by the city of San Antonio is a recent example of government overreach regarding this issue.

The ordinance reads, in part:

> "No appointed official or member of a board or commission shall engage in discrimination or demonstrate a bias, *by word or deed*, [emphasis added] against any person, group of persons, or organization on the basis of race, color, religion, national origin, sex, sexual orientation, gender identity, veteran status, age, or disability, while acting in their official capacity while in such public position."

The use of the phrase "by word or deed" has raised a red flag among religious groups since gay activists have shown a penchant for aggressively suing or publicly ridiculing anyone who disagrees with gay marriage or who speaks publicly regarding a religious objection to homosexuality.

Dr. Frank Turek, for example, was abruptly fired from both Bank of America and Cisco Systems in 2011 after someone Googled his name and discovered he had written a book entitled *Correct, Not Politically Correct: How Same-Sex Marriage Hurts Everyone*. Although Turek never discussed his views at work, he was told that his beliefs were inconsistent with Cisco's tolerance policies and could not be tolerated.[12]

Rather than the scenario Maddow describes, it seems much more likely that supporters of traditional marriage will be vulnerable to job termination than will gays and lesbians. Meanwhile, African Americans are still battling workplace discrimination, both overt and subtle.

Brenda Howard experienced the millennial brand of subtle racism that is common today. In a commentary published in the Aug. 16, 2013 edition of *The Washington Post*, Howard described her emotional connection to Trayvon Martin's killing and the subsequent not-guilty verdict received by George Zimmerman. "I needed to do something" she wrote in response, and she decided to change the imagery on her computer desktop wallpaper.[13]

"I went to my job at a small doctor's office and made my computer desktop wallpaper (which was not viewable to the public) an image of a hoodie," wrote Howard. "It [was] meant as an acknowledgement that this senseless death had not gone unnoticed."[14]

Two weeks after placing the image on her computer, Howard's boss called her into his office. Apparently, some of her co-workers had complained and felt the image was inappropriate, although it could only be seen when she logged in or minimized all the windows open on her screen. Howard decided that, on principle, she could not take it down and left a job she had for six years.[15]

Howard's experience is an example of the restrictions placed on African Americans when it comes to self-expression in the workplace – from hairstyles, to fashion, to desktop photos or images. While others are often given wide latitude in terms of freedom of expression, blacks tend to be much more restricted, fearing that any expression may limit career advancement.

By comparison, gay activists believe that not being allowed to display family photos that include their same-sex partners on their desks at work is an act of discrimination, according to Ellen Sturtz, retired public servant and advocate for LGBT equality. Sturtz received media attention in June 2013 when she heckled First Lady Michelle Obama at a Democratic National Committee (DNC) fundraiser.[16]

In other words, they believe the freedom to express themselves as gay individuals extends to the workplace, and they are gaining ground on that front in many corporations. Meanwhile, it is a battle African Americans are still quietly fighting and gaining little traction.

Wrong About Jim Crow, Wrong About Everything

Another assertion by the media and gay activists is that if the majority culture was wrong about slavery, Jim Crow and interracial marriage, then that necessarily means those against gay marriage are wrong too. This contention is built on a shaky foundation that has no basis because it is worse than comparing apples to oranges. At least apples and oranges are both fruit.

An individual's race is genetic and immutable. Despite pronouncements by gay activists that all gays are "born that way," there is no "gay gene," no definitive scientific evidence of a genetic component to homosexuality. This notion will be discussed in greater detail in Chapter 5.

For anyone who claims there is no difference between the histories of blacks and homosexuals and how both groups are impacted in the present, one need only reference the multitude of instances where a generic black man is falsely accused of a crime so the real culprit can escape detection by the authorities. Or an unarmed black teenager is killed by someone who perceives him to be "suspicious" and later claims the killing was in self-defense and is acquitted. This simply doesn't happen to homosexuals because their sexual preference is not usually apparent to the casual observer.

Yet, that did not stop MSNBC hosts Thomas Roberts and Rachel Maddow from cleverly weaving attacks against gays into their coverage of the unfortunate shooting of Trayvon Martin in Florida. Following the not-guilty verdict of George Zimmerman, the man on trial for killing Martin, Roberts used his morning broadcast to promote the idea that Martin being labeled "suspicious" by Zimmerman was similar to what gays experience when they are perceived as "other."

Maddow opened her July 15, 2013 program by discussing the Texas killing of James Byrd Jr. and one of the men who ultimately received the death penalty for the murder. She then used the Byrd story and connected it to Matthew Shepard, a gay man in Wyoming who was beaten and left for dead by two assailants. Shepard died from his wounds a few days later and his murder is considered to be one of most notorious murders of a gay man in American history.

Interestingly, the murders of Shepard and Byrd were intertwined to enact legislation which created penalties for hate crimes against LGBT individuals. Byrd was not a homosexual, but his murder led to the enactment of the Matthew Shepard and James Byrd Jr. Hate Crimes Prevention Act in 2009, most frequently referred to as the Matthew Shepard Act. The Act was signed into law by President Barack Obama.

Despite Roberts' and Maddow's attempts to connect the experiences of LGBT individuals to those of black males, the two have little to nothing in common. Gay men are not subjected to "stop and frisk" searches or handcuffed face down on sidewalks by police officers, something young black men experience all too often. Gay men do not receive harsher prison sentences when compared to individuals from other groups. Gay men are not automatically assumed to be "suspicious" or "dangerous" by the mainstream society unless, of course, they are black. They don't have problems hailing cabs in major cities. Women don't clutch their purses when a gay man enters an elevator, nor lock their doors when a gay man walks by. Again, their sexual orientation is largely unknown to the casual observer and is not an issue in terms of profiling or stereotyping.

How has the use of black oppression as a foil for gay marriage gone unchallenged for so long? There are a number of reasons.

Ignorance of History

First, many Americans are either uninformed or in denial regarding the nearly 400-year history of brutality and degradation African-Americans and their ancestors have experienced. Unless one selects African-American history as a college major, enrolls in extensive course study in this discipline, or makes a personal decision to research and study this aspect of U.S. history, there is little information provided in basic history courses or through mass media.

In public school textbooks, slavery is mentioned in a few brief paragraphs with very little detail, discussions of Reconstruction and Jim Crow are given short shrift, and present-day discrimination is virtually ignored. In bookstores, including the nation's largest bookstore chain, Barnes & Noble, books on American slavery are not included in the U.S. History section, but are relegated to African-American Studies or Cultural Studies.

Black History Month has been reduced to a recitation of Martin Luther King's "I Have a Dream" speech and a listing of the "first black" inventors and achievers. Simply put, gay activists have been able to take advantage of the American populace's dearth of knowledge.

The truly ugly side of our nation's history as it relates to African Americans is simply unspoken. Certainly, the unique, horrific legacy of African Americans is too painful for many to recall and discuss, but to pretend that it is the equivalent of an individual's or group's same-gender sexual attraction is not only inaccurate, it is insulting to the millions of African Americans who are the descendants of slaves.

Indeed, promoting homosexuality would certainly not have been part of the historic civil rights agenda because its organizations were headed by pastors. The Southern Christian Leadership Conference (SCLC), an organization founded by King to coordinate protest and civil rights activities in the South, was comprised almost exclusively of Protestant pastors in its upper ranks. Local churches became the central meeting places and launching pads for most of the protest actions during the Movement. When students in North Carolina and South Carolina implemented sit-ins to integrate lunch counters in major department stores, they met at church first and then peacefully marched downtown to the stores where their protests began.[17]

In addition, operating with a degree of unquestionable moral character was a major qualification for any leadership role in the movement. Martin Luther King Jr., in fact, encouraged African Americans to raise their standards of morality. "The first thing about life is that any man can be good and honest and ethical in morals, and have character," said King in the late 1950s.[18]

Much has been written about King's supposed sexual dalliances and alleged adulterous affairs. But King clearly knew that what he was doing was wrong because he went to great lengths to keep his private affairs private. Whatever his shortcomings, King did not flaunt his mistakes and try to justify them.

Moreover, although Rosa Parks is widely considered to be the mother of the Civil Rights Movement, she was not the first black woman who refused to give up her seat on a Montgomery, Ala., city bus. Another young black woman, Claudette Colvin, was arrested before Parks. However, Parks had an unblemished reputation, a respectable trade as a seamstress and was secretary of the local chapter of the National Association for the Advancement of Colored People (NAACP). Colvin, conversely, was a pregnant high school student who had used profanity when she was arrested for disobeying bus segregation laws. In other words, Colvin was not considered to be of adequate moral character to be the national symbol of the Montgomery bus boycott.

Some gay activists point to Bayard Rustin, a gay African American who was a little known, but important participant in the Civil Rights Movement, as evidence that Movement leaders had an affinity to the gay cause. However, since Rustin was also a Communist, his presence was a constant cause of anxiety for Movement leaders, the majority of whom were pastors.

Because of Rustin's dedication to civil rights, King and other Movement leaders chose to maintain Rustin's involvement, but there was always concern that his presence would completely derail the cause. In addition, Rustin's involvement was based upon the fact that he was an African American, not based on his sexual orientation. The Civil Rights Movement was for black rights and homosexuality as an issue was not on the agenda of the effort, one way or the other.

The reality is that King actually paid a price for befriending Rustin. King had planned to picket the 1960 Democratic Convention in Los Angeles in response to Southern opposition to the inclusion of a civil rights plank in the Democratic platform. Congressman Adam Clayton Powell (D-N.Y.) sent King a message that if he didn't call off the picket, Powell would tell the press that King was having a homosexual affair with Rustin.[19] The picketing proceeded but, to King's relief, Powell didn't follow through on his threat.

As a result of this situation, among others involving Rustin, and the internal resistance that had been building among preachers who were put off by his homosexuality and Communist past, King made the decision to break all contact with Rustin.[20]

These facts about Rustin's involvement in the Movement did not deter some members of the national media from presenting revisionist history by attempting to paint the 1963 March on Washington as some sort of coalition between gays and blacks. Georgetown University Professor and frequent television commentator Michael Eric Dyson attempted to tie the March on Washington to the push for gay marriage rhetorically. "Then he [King] was talking about economic inequality and social injustice. Now we're talking about gay and lesbian rights," said Dyson during an Aug. 26, 2013 interview on MSNBC. During coverage of the 50th anniversary of the March in August 2013, MSNBC, in particular, tried to elevate the fact that Rustin was gay by saying he was a "representative of the LBGT community," as if the March was some sort of gay pride rally.

Not only was there no politically organized LGBT community in 1963, as stated previously, Movement leaders went out of their way to hide Rustin's homosexuality because, if it had become known, their efforts would have been completely derailed. The purpose of the March on Washington and the larger Civil Rights Movement were to secure constitutional rights for African Americans. King made the focus of the Movement clear to observers during an interview with NBC's "Meet the Press" on Aug. 25, 1963, three days before the March. "The *Negro* [emphasis added] has been extremely patient. We have waited for well now 345 years for our basic constitutional and God-given rights," he said.

One minister who was intricately involved in the Movement said that some gay activists are rewriting history from the 1950s and 1960s and taking liberties with the facts. "A lot of people are doing things in Martin's name that he would never have been a part of," said Dr. Virgil A. Wood, in an April 21, 2013 address delivered at Fallbrook Church in Houston, Texas. Wood served with Dr. King for ten years as a member of his National Executive Board of the Southern Christian Leadership Conference (SCLC), and coordinated the state of Virginia for the March.

Wood says the idea of "marriage equality" is an absurd notion because of its obvious paradoxical elements. "The people arguing for marriage 'equality' would not exist if their parents had decided to marry someone of the same gender."

That appears to be the case for Susan Meander Tobias who wrote a commentary in the April 5, 2013 edition of *The Washington Post* titled, "My father's gay marriage." Tobias asserts that her father was gay, "doubtless born that way," and that his "very nature was criminal in 1950s and 1960s America."[21] Ironically, if Tobias had her way and her father was allowed to marry a man instead of her mother, she would not exist.

Rev. Fred Shuttlesworth, who died in 2011 and was one of King's closest allies, was also an outspoken opponent of homosexual behavior.[22]

African-American Political Leaders Have Divided Loyalties

The use of black oppression by gay activists has also gone unchallenged because, unfortunately, many African-American political leaders have compromised their principles. In one notable example, a black congressman attended a 2006 meeting of the Peninsula Baptist Pastors Council, an association of black pastors in the Tidewater, Virginia area. The congressman asked the ministers to vote against the referendum that would ban gay marriage. Sources at the meeting said the ministers were obviously stunned and offended, and one of them asked the congressman: "Do you go to the meetings of gay groups and ask them to support *our* agenda?" The congressman sheepishly answered, "No," a clear indication of where his loyalties lay.

The same question could be asked of President Barack Obama. Since his May 2012 public announcement that he had switched positions and favored gay marriage, whenever Obama addresses an African-American audience, he seems to mention his support for gay marriage, either directly or indirectly. Yet, when the president addresses gay organizations, I could find no instances where he mentions support for African-American equal rights or voting rights.

Public records from the Federal Election Commission (FEC) indicate that 80 percent of the members of the Congressional Black Caucus (CBC) have received campaign contributions from the Human Rights Campaign Fund (HRC), the largest, best-financed and most powerful gay political action committee in America.[23] Over the past decade, CBC members collectively received more than $600,000 in cash contributions from HRC. This money would not be donated if these politicians were not expected to support and advance the PAC's agenda. Sadly, there is no comparable black PAC to lobby for and protect the African-American community's interests and legacy.

The following members of Congress are the only members of the CBC who have *not* received financial backing from the HRC as of September 2013:

- Rep. Karen Bass (D-Calif.)
- Rep. Sanford Bishop (D-Ga.)
- Rep. Andre Carson (D-Ind.)
- Rep. Donna Christensen (D-V.I.)
- Rep. William Lacy Clay (D-Mo.)
- Rep. Cedric Richmond (D-La.)
- Rep. Terri Sewell (D-Ala.)
- Rep. Bennie Thompson (D-Miss.)

Only the politically naïve believe that large financial contributions do not affect votes or politicians' positions. Lobbying groups like HRC raise money to finance political campaigns. The purpose and goal of any lobbying group is to influence votes and to promote a particular agenda. The HRC's political action committee does not raise $1.5 million or more during each election cycle and dole it out to politicians because they like them. They expect something in return – support of a gay agenda – and they get it.

As is often the case, the members of the CBC are completely out of touch with the beliefs and principles of their constituents. The majority of black Americans do not agree that civil rights for blacks are comparable to equal rights for gays, according to a survey conducted by Zogby Analytics Polling in February 2013. Fifty-five percent of black respondents said the rights were not equivalent and another 17 percent said they were not sure. Only 28 percent of survey respondents agreed with the comparison.[24]

To be sure, black leaders should be given the benefit of the doubt that they are sincere in their belief that black civil rights and gay rights are equivalent. But they are likely influenced by the affinity blacks in general often have for the ill-treated and dispossessed. That was the motivation behind Rev. Osagyefo Uhuru Sekou's support for gay rights, even at the risk of potentially losing his credentials in the Church of God in Christ. Sekou is professor of preaching at the Seminary Consortium of Urban Pastoral Education in the Graduate Theological Urban Studies Program in Chicago. But, after 10 years working in support of gay rights causes, Sekou noted the glaring lack of reciprocal support for black civil rights causes by gay organizations.

"I must confess that I have shown up far more for gay marriage advocates than they have shown up for us [blacks]," he wrote in a blog post on the day the Supreme Court struck down DOMA. "The complicit silence of gay marriage advocates on issues of race and class oppression is deafening."[25]

It is obvious that Sekou and other black leaders did not thoroughly analyze the ramifications of a societal shift in the direction of equating same-gender marriage with traditional, heterosexual marriage. Nor did they adequately contemplate the repercussions of comparing the banning of gay marriage to African-American suffering. The results have been a monumental advancement in terms of the promotion of homosexuality and, in many cases, a rollback of black civil rights.

Pro-Gay Marriage African Americans Dominate On-Air Interviews

The third reason the hijacking of the Civil Rights Movement has been successful lies with the media's portrayal of African-American support for gay marriage, even though the reality is that the majority of blacks are either against it or are undecided. In fact, African Americans have been described as the "last Democratic holdouts on gay marriage" by some political observers.[26]

There have been a limited number of polls taken which have large enough sample sizes of African Americans to be credible. But three studies conducted in 2013 reveal that only about 40 percent of blacks are in favor of gay marriage. One was a March 2013 Pew Research Center study, which compiled results from four surveys conducted over more than a year.²⁷ The Pew Center conducted another survey two months later with similar results.²⁸ The other was an extensive study of African-American political opinion commissioned by Robert L. Johnson, founder and former president of Black Entertainment Television (BET), in February 2013.²⁹ Religious attitudes help explain some of this opposition as African-Americans tend to be more religious than the American population as a whole.³⁰

A recent example of how this difference within the Democratic Party of relatively low African-American support for gay marriage was demonstrated in the November 2012 election. Gay marriage was approved by Maryland voters but narrowly rejected in predominantly black Prince George's County, a deeply Democratic part of the state that includes many large religious institutions. At the same time, President Obama received the support of 90 percent of Prince George's County voters.³¹

Despite the fact that most African Americans do not support gay marriage, for most of their on-camera interviews on this topic, media select African Americans who support it. Among their favorite interviewees are the following:

- Rev. Al Sharpton, National Action Network
- Rev. Jesse Jackson, Rainbow PUSH Coalition
- Benjamin Jealous, president and CEO, NAACP
- Julian Bond, former chairman of the NAACP
- Cory Booker, mayor of Newark, N.J.
- Michael Eric Dyson, professor, Georgetown University
- Joy-Ann Reid, managing editor, TheGrio.com

- Melissa Harris-Perry, TV talk show host
- Touré, writer and TV co-host
- Keith Boykin, MSNBC/CNBC contributor, author, gay activist
- Jonathan Capehart, *Washington Post* columnist
- Wes Moore, U.S. Army veteran, author and political commentator
- Tavis Smiley, talk show host and author
- Jamal Simmons, political commentator and consultant
- Members of the Congressional Black Caucus, 80 percent of whom receive funds from the Human Rights Campaign, the most powerful gay lobbying group in the nation

Since media limit their interviews almost exclusively to African Americans who favor gay marriage, it gives the public the false impression that the majority of blacks do also. In fact, it is quite deceptive because this portrayal is not at all representative of what the majority of black people actually think.

Convoluted Comparison Highlights Failures on Political Left and Right

Finally, the convoluted comparison between gay rights and black civil rights has been possible due to failings on both the political left and right. On the left, 1960s liberals express a sense of pride in having supported equal rights for African Americans. But most of them are apparently unable to distinguish between the centuries-long brutality and disenfranchisement of America's black citizens and the more recent discomfort and humiliation experienced by gays who would like to or have already come out of the closet.

Apparently, in the liberal view, all suffering is equal. The person who has sprained his ankle should receive the same medical attention as the pedestrian hit by a moving 18-wheeler. In their minds, there are no distinctions between one victim and another.

On the right, for far too long, most conservatives stood in the way of any reasonable pursuit of equal treatment under the law for African Americans. In their view, there was no need to ensure the right to vote, remove the intimidating "colored only" and "white only" signs," or provide decent educational facilities for black children. Many defended flying the Confederate flag when they knew it was and still remains to be a symbol of racial intimidation and violence. They could not be persuaded otherwise, and many still harbor the belief that blacks are inherently inferior.

I will admit that I am personally conflicted with the idea that, on this issue, I am politically aligned with some people who still do not believe in equal rights for African Americans. Yet, I have to put those thoughts aside to stand firm on a principle that I know is not only better for African Americans, but for society as a whole. And just because many conservatives have been wrong on race, doesn't mean they are wrong about everything. After all, if a conservative (or a liberal) individual discovered the cure for cancer, would I reject the treatment because of his political views?

That is why I became politically independent over a decade ago. I found it impossible to stand on my principles and consistently fit comfortably in either major party.

But the sad truth is that many conservatives have been so wrong-headed on the issue of race that when gays raise the issue as a challenge to their views on homosexuality, most do not have a moral leg to stand on. Sensing this vulnerability, gay activists have cleverly used this as a way to intimidate and thus neutralize evangelical Christians, most of whom are politically conservative, when it comes to the issue of homosexuality being sanctioned by the government.

Pricking America's Moral Consciousness

The goal of the Civil Rights Movement was to prick the moral consciousness of America. Even after all that America had done to African Americans, its leaders believed that if Americans could see their fellow Negro (as they were referred to at that time) citizens as peaceful people who wanted nothing more than to be treated as equals under the law, they would be moved to act.

King and the Movement's other leaders gave no thought to raising money to finance politicians' campaigns and influence their votes. They believed that media exposure of their non-violent protests -- and the predictably violent response by their adversaries -- would be enough to persuade those who were sitting on the proverbial fence.

The cruel irony is that, if gay rights advocates succeed in legalizing gay marriage nationwide, the same churches that gave birth to the Civil Rights Movement may be forced by the government to perform marriage ceremonies that are antithetical to Biblical and moral principles, or be penalized with fines, loss of funding for social programs, or by having their tax exempt status revoked.

This legacy is completely lost on media representatives as they have all, in one cacophonous voice, followed the gay marriage advocates' lead and compared laws against interracial marriage between whites and blacks (which were still traditional male/female unions, by the way), to the movement to redefine marriage as any union of two consenting adults, regardless of gender.

Racial Discrimination Within LGBT Community

Media also fail to acknowledge or report on the racism and lack of diversity within the lesbian-gay-bisexual-transgender (LGBT) ranks. Television talk show host Roland Martin, on TV One's program "Washington Watch," interviewed the heads of three black gay rights organizations on March 11, 2013: Rev. Darlene Nipper, deputy executive director of the National Gay and Lesbian Task Force; Cleo Manago, CEO and founder of Black Men's Xchange; and Earl Fowlkes, president and CEO of the Center for Black Equity. All three spokespeople said blacks had been largely excluded from LGBT discussions and finances, and that, on many occasions, were subjected to racial slurs.

The discrimination which occurs within the LGBT community is a phenomenon about which media are either unaware or have made a conscious decision to ignore. Reporting on instances where LGBT activists have been hypocritical when it comes to discriminating against others does not fit into the media's narrative that every gay individual is a victim, and could not possibly be an aggressor in terms of relationships with blacks or heterosexuals.

The media's wholehearted adoption of the black Civil Rights Movement as a gateway to gay marriage rights paved the way for a softening of resistance to these unions and played a major role in the resultant shift in public opinion polls. Without the use of black suffering as a foil, it is doubtful that gay activists would have convinced a majority of Americans to move in the direction of gay marriage as a "civil right."

Clearly, homosexuals have experienced discrimination and ill treatment. But they made a decision long ago that instead of telling their story, they would piggyback on the story of African-American racial suffering and use that as a stepping stone to victory. The media have been equal participants in that effort.

CHAPTER 2
STACKING THE DECK

The media's promotion of gay marriage may have started with the comparison with black civil rights, but it didn't end there. Long ago, media abandoned any pretense that their coverage reflected the almost equally-divided attitudes of the American populace concerning gay marriage. Instead, they decided to stack the deck in favor of same-sex marriage, consistently presenting lineups where their guest panels were clearly one-sided.

Media began presenting this one-sided coverage even when the majority of Americans opposed gay marriage, so it has not been a recent development. But it is my view that the majority of individuals consuming the news are completely unaware of this imbalance, instead believing that the entire country has actually jumped aboard the gay marriage bandwagon.

If there were any doubts regarding the mainstream media's stance on gay marriage, these doubts were squelched during coverage following the Supreme Court's rulings on the Defense of Marriage Act (DOMA) and California's Proposition 8. CNN, in particular, has positioned itself as the moderate television news network when compared to the liberal-leaning MSNBC and the conservative-leaning Fox. Yet, during the daytime news programming on June 26, 2013, the 24-hour news network included three times as many on-air guests supporting the Supreme Court's gay marriage decisions as opposing them, according to a study conducted by the Media Research Center. The prime time coverage that evening was even more lopsided than it was during the day. From 5 to 9 p.m. EST, thirteen guests supporting the same-sex marriage rulings appeared on CNN, compared to only two opponents.[32]

In the wake of the Supreme Court rulings regarding gay marriage, Jack Mirkinson of the *Huffington Post* wrote a column about the increased visibility of gay journalists on news broadcasts. "The opponents of gay marriage were almost nowhere to be seen, either on the TV screen or the websites or the newspapers," he wrote, describing the June 26th news coverage. Mirkinson's implication was that gay marriage opponents did not exist or that their influence had been so diminished that they were ashamed to be seen publicly. The truth is that their opinions were elicited by the media in much smaller numbers than those who favor same-sex unions.[33]

On the June 30, 2013 broadcast of ABC's "This Week" with George Stephanopoulos, the host did have a balanced panel with Chad Griffin, president of the HRC, and Brian Brown, president of NOM. But Stephanopoulos began the program by enthusiastically congratulating Griffin on his victory, letting the audience know where the host's allegiances lay.

Slots for television news programs are not selected at random. The producers carefully screen guests beforehand with intense telephone interviews to determine their perspective. The producers' preference is to include guests who have strong opinions on either side of an issue so there can be a vigorous debate.

Moreover, within the mainstream media outlets, one would be hard pressed to find more than one or two on-air TV hosts, or behind-the-scenes producers, who are not in favor of gay marriage or, at the very least, completely silent on the issue. In fact, with the exception of Fox News, the ranks of on-air personalities is so devoid of individuals who oppose gay marriage -- despite the fact that nearly half the country holds the same position -- that one could surmise the question may even be alluded to during the job interview process. Or that the social media histories of potential applicants were examined by human resource personnel in advance to ensure that no individuals in opposition to gay marriage were considered for on-air positions. Or that perhaps those who are opposed do not even apply for positions because they know they do not have a snowball's chance in Hades of being hired.

The truth is that, for years, opponents of gay marriage have been excluded from on-air discussions of this issue or have been included primarily for the purpose of being publicly ridiculed by the host and one or more pro-gay marriage advocates. Watch any so-called debate on the topic of gay marriage on programs like MSNBC's "Hardball with Chris Matthews," CNN's "Piers Morgan" or "Anderson Cooper 360" and it is obvious there is a tag team with the host and the gay marriage advocate(s) on one side, and the supporter of traditional marriage on the other. The concept of a neutral moderator or host has been completely discarded.

The examples are too numerous to enumerate them all but, in addition to the obviously lopsided coverage on the day the Supreme Court handed down the DOMA and Proposition 8 rulings, here are just a few. On March 25, 2013, CNN anchor Don Lemon, who publicly announced in 2011 that he was openly gay, interviewed two guests regarding the Supreme Court's review of same-sex legal cases. The guests were CNN opinion columnist John Sutter, who was in favor of gay marriage, and Ryan Anderson of the Heritage Foundation, who was opposed. Anderson argued that gay marriage is not illegal, since if an act is illegal, a person can be incarcerated for committing it. Anderson also argued that children do best in households where a female mother and male father are married to each other, a fact that has been supported by every credible child development study conducted.

During the seven-minute interview, Lemon became so frustrated with Anderson's assertions that he spent the entire segment arguing with his Heritage Foundation guest, rather than allowing both of his guests to have equal time. Meanwhile, Sutter, who was still on camera, simply smiled since Lemon, the host, was doing his work for him. Even though it was a two-against-one conversation and he was outnumbered, Anderson actually seemed to have the upper hand when the segment's time had expired. The entire interview can be viewed via YouTube here: http://www.youtube.com/watch?v=9aijl-fEw8Y

Another example of the media's stacking the deck occurred on NBC's "Meet the Press," the world's longest running television program. The March 31, 2013 edition featured a panel on the issue of gay marriage in the aftermath of the U.S. Supreme Court hearing arguments earlier that week. The panel was moderated by Chuck Todd, who substituted for the usual host, David Gregory. Based on Todd's remarks on previous MSNBC programs, it is clear that he supports gay marriage. The guest panelists included:

- Rev. Al Sharpton – Pro-gay marriage
- Pete Williams – Legal correspondent, openly gay
- Rob Reiner – Hollywood actor, gay marriage advocate
- Peggy Noonan – Newspaper columnist and author, neutral on gay marriage
- Brian Brown – President of National Organization for Marriage (NOM), opposed to gay marriage

Including Todd, four of the six people who appeared on the program were in support of gay marriage, one was neutral and one was opposed. Although Noonan's career has been as a commentator from a moderate to conservative point of view, during this particular broadcast she provided no opinion on gay marriage, one way or the other. Brown was the only guest who was invited by the show's producers to present an opposing viewpoint.

Regarding the "Meet the Press" episode, the producers did something during Brown's on-camera comments that they did not do for the other guests: They included a graphic about Brown's religious affiliation, noting that he was a former Quaker who later converted to Roman Catholicism. The producers also included the size of his family in the graphic, noting that he had eight children.

Interestingly, this information was not provided for Rob Reiner, the other non-media guest. Reiner is Jewish and, according to his online biographical information, he has three children. But the producers apparently did not believe these facts were important because they failed to include them in the graphic which appeared adjacent to his camera shot. One can only conclude that the producers informed viewers about Brown's religion and the size of his family to create a bias against him and his political position. The "Meet the Press" episode described above, which includes Brown, Reiner and others, can be viewed online via YouTube here: http://www.youtube.com/watch?v=Mvqtd26Zkvk

The next day on Todd's MSNBC program, "The Daily Rundown," he had an on-air discussion with his guests about the concept of marriage being redefined. "Marriage gets redefined all the time," was his retort. However, Todd is simply wrong. Marriage in the U.S. has never been redefined to be a same-gender institution, nor has it been for the vast majority of countries around the world.

CNN's Piers Morgan has publicly pronounced his support for gay marriage by calling for a "gay marriage amendment to the Bible." He is among the most abusive of the television hosts when he has any guest on his show who opposes gay marriage, using words like "bizarre" and "un-American" for those who believe in traditional male/female marriage. Apparently, he does not believe that those who are opposed to gay marriage deserve even the slightest modicum of cordiality or respect, as evidenced by the March 26, 2013 discussion with financial guru Suze Orman, who is gay, and Ryan Anderson of NOM.

Morgan's treatment of Anderson could aptly be described as bizarre, and he seemed to want to make the traditional marriage advocate pay a price for appearing on his program. Rather than have Anderson sit at the interview table with him and Orman, Morgan positioned Anderson several feet away in a group of studio participants, as if the NOM representative was radioactive. Morgan's message was clear: Anderson should be shunned and treated like a pariah for his beliefs.

To reinforce this imbalance of opinion, members of the mainstream media put a tremendous amount of resources into emphasizing stories that advance the cause of legalizing gay marriage. Television broadcasters don't limit coverage to a single news report, but will make these stories the topics of discussion on continuous evening network talk shows, one after the next.

Thus, on CNN, a segment will appear on Erin Burnett's "Outfront," then on Anderson Cooper's "360," then on "Piers Morgan Live," then all three programs are re-broadcast later in the evening. On MSNBC, a segment will appear on "The Ed Show" with Ed Schultz, then on Al Sharpton's "Politics Nation," then on "Hardball With Chris Matthews," then on "All In With Chris Hayes," then on "The Rachel Maddow Show," and finally on "The Last Word with Lawrence O'Donnell." Most of the shows are then rebroadcast for the network's late-night programming.

Print Media Stack the Deck Too

One stacking-the-deck technique used by print media is to create a headline using the opinion of a gay advocate, knowing that headlines are all a majority of consumers will read or remember. A good example is a March 7, 2013 article in the *Los Angeles Times* with the headline, "Opposition to Same-Sex Marriage Increasingly Isolated, Pollsters Say." It is not until they get to paragraph five that readers discover that the pollsters to which the headline refers performed the analysis for Freedom to Marry, a leading advocacy group for same-sex marriage. The poll was not conducted by a neutral polling firm and, thus, its questions and intent had a built-in bias.[34]

In addition, the headline implies that those who oppose gay marriage live in the hinterlands, lacking access to state-of-the-art technology and disconnected from modern society. The fact is that 70 percent of Americans live in states where gay marriage is banned or where marriage between a man and a woman has been codified into the states' constitutions.

A second approach used by print media is to utilize headlines which are either misleading or incomplete. During the Pope's trip to Brazil in July 2013, for example, when he made statements regarding homosexuality during an impromptu press conference on the airplane, the Pontiff described his beliefs regarding gay individuals. Most headlines were similar to the one utilized by CBS News: "Pope Francis On Gays: Who Am I To Judge?"[35]

Yet, the Pope said a whole lot more that could have easily been included in a headline, such as his belief that engaging in homosexual acts is a sin. The Pope also made reference to lobbying efforts by gay groups. "The problem is not having this orientation. We must be brothers. The problem is lobbying by this orientation, or lobbies of greedy people, political lobbies, Masonic lobbies, so many lobbies. This is the worst problem," he said.[36]

However, the media chose to promote only the portions of the Pope's press conference that were favorable to gay activists. While the Pope's comments were indeed conciliatory, this decision by the media left the public with the impression that the Pope could possibly be in favor of gay marriage. Clearly, based on the totality of his remarks, this would not have been the case.

Another tactic used by print media is to goad politicians and other individuals who oppose gay marriage into changing their position. Chris Cillizza, who writes "The Fix," a daily political weblog on the *Washington Post* website, used this approach in his June 27, 2013 column titled, "A majority of the country supports gay marriage. Will any 2016 Republican presidential candidate?" In the column, Cillizza, my fellow Georgetown University alumnus (although he graduated a few years after I did), asserts, "Opposing the right of gay people to marry is, increasingly, a losing political proposition."[37] He repeated his assertion the next day when he appeared on MSNBC as a substitute host for Chuck Todd's "The Daily Rundown."

Cillizza's evidence: He provides none, because recent national, statewide and Congressional elections have not hinged upon a politician's approval of gay marriage. To date, there has not been one high profile political race where a candidate's approval of gay marriage was the determining factor in the election. Support for gay marriage may be an essential position for most Democratic politicians, but Republicans who switch positions may actually be in jeopardy. And Cillizza ignores the fact that New Jersey Governor Chris Christie opposes gay marriage and his approval ratings among New Jersey residents are among the highest of any governor in the country.

Some print media outlets have stretched the boundaries of what was once considered to be journalistic standards and engaged in activities which were once believed to be antithetical to their profession. Thomas Reuters, parent of the journalism powerhouse Reuters news agency, joined a coalition of companies that favored repealing the Defense of Marriage Act.[38] Viacom, another media behemoth, was also a participant.[39] In essence, Reuters and Viacom made financial investments in a group advocating for a specific political issue, rather than remain unbiased as has been the time-honored tradition of media entities.

Stacking the deck in favor of the pro-gay marriage position, coupled with the rudeness, name-calling and double standards for those who are opposed, has three chilling effects. First, those in opposition to gay marriage will be wary of accepting invitations for television and newspaper interviews for fear of being metaphorically raked over the coals. Individuals rarely volunteer to be the recipients of verbal attacks or ideological ambushes.

Second, although this skewed media coverage is a completely inaccurate portrayal of the attitudes of the American electorate, it creates a bandwagon effect. Some people who are undecided about gay marriage will actually switch positions because they believe the proverbial train has already left the station. This further distorts the polling results as those who are actually still vacillating are included within the group that solidly supports the practice. Third, and more importantly, it gives the audience the false impression that those in opposition to gay marriage are few in number.

In reality, although the mainstream media gives the impression that the country is overwhelmingly in support of gay marriage, polling data reflect a much more evenly split populace. Polling results differ based on the questions that are asked of the respondents.

Brian Brown, president of NOM, says the use of specific language can make a real difference. "The whole 'illegal' thing summons the wrong sort of impressions in respondents," he said in an interview with the *Washington Post*. "You're loading the question. The illegal language brings the specter of enforcement."[40]

Most polls on this topic ask the question in legal/illegal terms. A much-cited ABC-*Washington Post* poll released in March 2013 asked whether "it should be legal or illegal for gay and lesbian couples to get married." Fifty-eight percent of those polled said "legal." This poll was clearly an outlier, since other polls conducted during the same time frame showed results in the low 50s for the legal/illegal question.[41]

But that did not keep media representatives, like MSNBC's Chris Matthews, from using it as an example of the nation's supposed overwhelming shift in favor of gay marriage. Matthews completely ignored the existence of the Pew Research poll that was released the same week and showed support at only 49 percent.[42]

When respondents are queried in terms of the definition of marriage, the results are much more evenly divided. An NBC News/*Wall Street Journal* poll released in April 2013 asked the following question: "If there were a federal standard defining marriage across the country, would you prefer it include same-sex marriage in the definition of marriage or define marriage as between one man and one woman?" Forty-eight percent of respondents said marriage should be defined as between one man and one woman, 47 percent said it should include same-sex marriages and 5 percent were not sure.[43]

Similarly, a *Huffington Post* poll conducted May 30-31, 2013 showed that more Americans want the federal government to define marriage as between one man and one woman (45 percent) than want it redefined to include people of either gender (43 percent).[44] *The Huffington Post* is a liberal media outlet, so the results of its poll are not insignificant.

The media's penchant for stacking the deck of on-air guests in favor of gay marriage presents an inaccurate portrait of where voters actually stand on this issue. Rather than reflect a country which is nearly evenly divided, news coverage is much more lopsided. Perhaps they believe that if those who oppose gay marriage were provided with any semblance of equitable treatment by the media, more people would be willing to re-examine their positions or even shift their support for marriage as it has been defined since the dawn of modern civilization.

More information about polling results and how media manipulate them to persuade undecided voters will be explored in Chapter 12.

CHAPTER 3
CARROTS AND STICKS

In addition to stacking the deck in favor of gay marriage when the issue is discussed on news programs, the media also utilize a carrot-and-stick approach to persuade more people to support gay marriage. The concept of carrots and sticks refers to a system of rewards and punishments, often utilized in management systems and in politics. The carrot represents the incentive or reward; the stick represents the punishment. This term, developed in the late 1800s, alludes to enticing a horse or donkey to move by dangling a carrot before it and, either alternately or at the same time, urging the animal forward by beating it with a stick.[45]

Utilizing the carrot-and-stick concept, media publicly reward politicians and others who publicly support gay marriage. Conversely, they punish those in opposition.

Positive media coverage for politicians is not easy to come by, as the vast majority of news stories covering elected officials are either negative or neutral. But when politicians announce their support for gay marriage, they are almost guaranteed as least one news cycle of positive media coverage.

When former Secretary of State Hillary Clinton made her public announcement that she was switching her position in support of gay marriage, on March 18, 2013 through a video released by the Human Rights Campaign, the positive media coverage triggered a near avalanche of other mostly-Democratic politicians switching sides.

Senator Claire McKaskill (D-Mo.) announced her support on March 24, followed by Senators Mark Warner (D-Va.) and Mark Begich (D-Alaska) on March 25, Sen. Jon Tester (D-MT) on March 26, Sen. Kay Hagan (D-N.C.) on March 27, Sen. Bob Casey (D-Pa.) on April 1, Senators Tom Carper (D-Del.) and Mark Kirk (R-Ill.) on April 2, Sen. Bill Nelson (D-Fla.) on April 4, and Senators Heidi Heitkamp (D-N.D.) and Joe Donnelly (D-Ind.) on April 5. All of these senators received positive national media coverage on the days their announcements were made.[46]

On April 5, MSNBC's Thomas Roberts referred to Democratic senators as "falling like dominoes" in changing their position on gay marriage. "Who are the holdouts?" he asked, putting obvious pressure on those who still opposed the redefinition of marriage. On April 8, Sen. Tim Johnson (D-S.D.) decided that he was ready to take the plunge and announced he was switching positions too. The only three Democratic senators who have not switched positions as of September 2013 are Mark Pryor of Arkansas, Mary Landrieu of Louisiana, and Joe Manchin of West Virginia. All three represent states that President Obama lost in both the 2008 and 2012 elections.[47]

Media also reward high-profile gay individuals who come out of the closet. The rewards are dispensed through the glowing national media coverage they receive. In fact, there is currently no downside to a gay individual coming out of the closet and, in fact, it can be quite profitable, as demonstrated by recent events. Here are just some of the perks media and others dole out to those who publicly announce they are gay:

- Glowing, non-critical media coverage. No questions that are even remotely critical are asked as the usual objective of providing "balanced" coverage is abandoned.
- Instant fame. The individual receives coverage on all major networks, national magazines and newspapers.
- Kudos from sitting and former presidents. The individual is praised for bravery and receives personal calls from top political leaders.
- Book deals, record deals and/or movie roles.
- Increased income from endorsement deals or contract extensions.
- Large cadre of people who will defend what they are doing and everything they've ever done, while simultaneously attacking anyone who disagrees.

Jason Collins, Poster Child for Media Rewards

The poster child for this system of rewards is Jason Collins, the National Basketball Association (NBA) player who came out of the closet in April 2013 and was celebrated as the first openly gay male athlete still active in a major American team sport. Collins, a free agent who played on five other NBA teams before joining the Washington Wizards, was a little-known center who averaged only three points per game. In fact, most Americans had never heard of Collins before he came out of the closet as a gay man to public fanfare. And the media coverage was of a caliber about which only few can dream.

Collins graced the cover of the May 6, 2013 edition of *Sports Illustrated* with the headline "The Gay Athlete." The article told Collins' story, in his own words, regarding his journey as a gay man, those within his family with whom he first shared his secret, and some of the milestones he experienced along the way. There were no questions or critiques from the *Sports Illustrated* reporters, nor analysis of his confession. There was no attempt to write a "balanced" story, a description reporters often proffer when they interview those who are likely to have something critical to say about the subject of a feature article. *Sports Illustrated* provided Collins with what could only be described as a "puff piece."

Within a few days after Collins' announcement, he received personal phone calls from both President Obama and former President Bill Clinton, praising him for his courage in coming out of the closet. Nearly every major newspaper and news magazine featured the 34-year-old Collins in articles about what a breakthrough his "coming out" was for athletics. Oprah filmed a one-hour interview with Collins' entire family and aired it on her OWN network, and he was also interviewed on ABC's "Good Morning America."

According to David Lavin, the president of the Lavin Agency Speakers Bureau, Collins will be in "high demand" on the well-paying speaking circuit, especially at colleges and universities. Such speaking engagements can be particularly lucrative.[48]

Collins received the Courage Award from the Gay, Lesbian and Straight Education Network[49] and headlined a Democratic National Committee (DNC) LGBT Leadership fundraising gala with First Lady Michelle Obama.[50] There was talk of a potential book deal, although it had not yet materialized at the time this book went to press. Collins was ranked number 68 on *Guardian* magazine's World Pride Power List of the 100 Most Influential LGBT People for 2013.[51]

Collins demonstrates that a public announcement that one is homosexual is now a boost to one's career. An individual who has had a low public profile can be immediately catapulted to celebrity status.

Although Collins and other gay individuals claim they don't want their sexual orientation to be an issue, it seems that, for Collins, it may be the only issue that can be used to further his basketball career, since his performance on the court garnered him little recognition. He was described as a "lower-tier player" in a *New York Times* article three months after his coming out debut.

Collins has not been a full-time starter in six years, and the *Times* indicated he was the type of player teams "often seek in a 14th or 15th man." His status as a free agent was on hold as he remained unsigned, a situation he faced in previous seasons as the signing deadline approached. Yet, the *Times,* contended, if Collins is not signed, it "could be interpreted as a setback for gays in general."[52]

It's hard to see why a 34-year-old benchwarmer not being re-signed in the NBA is a setback or an extraordinary event. If Collins genuinely wants to be judged for his skills and not his orientation, he cannot expect that the fact that he is gay would give him points in the evaluation process. But in light of the lack of criticism Collins received from the media in the throes of his coming out celebration, he might be under the impression that using his orientation as a means of crying "foul" will work in his favor.

There are a number of questions media could have asked Collins after reading his *Sports Illustrated* confession if they were exhibiting their usual level of inquisitiveness. In the article, Collins wrote, "I can't wait to start a family of my own."[53] The first question that comes to the readers' minds – the big elephant in the room – is how does Collins plan to start a family with another man? The readers were left hanging.

Since he is gay and, by definition, cannot biologically produce a child with a male partner, how does he plan to get the family started? Will he adopt or use a surrogate mother? Or perhaps his partner, having changed his mind about his orientation after producing a child with a female, will bring children to their relationship. Advances in technology have afforded homosexuals opportunities to procreate which their sexual orientation otherwise would not.

Media cannot use the excuse that the questions might have been too intrusive, since there are few questions, especially those which are personal in nature, media representatives will not ask.

They delve into the private lives of public figures on a regular basis without hesitation.

Another issue Collins raised in the *Sports Illustrated* article was his Christian faith, as he indicated that his parents instilled Christian values during his upbringing. Then he adds, "I take the teachings of Jesus seriously, particularly the ones that touch on tolerance and understanding."[54]

Far be it for me to question any individual's commitment to faith and family. But this selective adoption of Jesus' teachings is common among gay activists and their supporters, who seem to limit their Bible reading to a handful of scriptures about love, tolerance and helping the poor. Meanwhile, they ignore all of Jesus' admonitions about the structure of marriage (male/female), the avoidance of sin, denying selfish desires, and the example of living a holy, righteous lifestyle.

Approaching Christianity this way is similar to an individual who desires to become a martial arts expert, but limits his instruction only to those lessons that deal with kicking. Meanwhile, he eschews the other core aspects of the discipline, which include breathing, focusing, self-defense, meditating, punching, pinning and physical fitness. Or, to use a basketball analogy, it would be the equivalent of a player only learning to dribble, and refusing lessons on shooting, passing, blocking and defending.

However, the most obvious question media refused to ask and which was left unanswered was the nature of Collins' long-term engagement to Carolyn Moos. According to Moos, the couple dated for eight years and she did not know he was gay until he told her the morning he came out to the world in the *Sports Illustrated* article. "A month before I was set to marry the man I loved, he called off the wedding," said Moos in a *USA Today* interview. "I had no idea why. . .We had planned to have children, build a family."[55]

Indeed, this depth of years-long deception is a reflection of deficits in Collins' character as well as his lack of honesty. Moos seemed to agree, as she had this critique of her former fiancé: "He's being hailed as a pioneer, but I believe true heroism is a result of being honest with yourself and with those you love."[56] Yet, media, apparently caught up in the euphoria of yet another gay individual coming out of the closet, asked Collins no critical questions whatsoever.

And those who challenged the veracity of Collins' statements were quickly rebuked. Here is where the "sticks" aspect of the "carrots and sticks" concept comes into play. Media critic Howard Kurtz lost his job as a columnist at the *Daily Beast* for writing that Collins had "left one little part out" of his *Sports Illustrated* piece: "He was engaged. To be married. To a woman." Collins did mention his engagement in the article, but he downplayed it so much that any reader could have easily overlooked it.[57]

The *Daily Beast* claimed Kurtz's firing was a result of the Collins snafu being the latest among a long list of infractions. "Tina Brown, editor in chief of both *Newsweek* and the *Daily Beast*, had been looking for a way to get rid of him for months," wrote *Forbes* staffer Jeff Berdovici in an article about Kurtz's infraction.⁵⁸ Interestingly, the *Daily Beast* is owned by IAC, whose chairman, Barry Diller, is gay.⁵⁹

But Kurtz was not allowed to say anything remotely critical about Collins, the newly-anointed media darling, without experiencing serious career repercussions. He issued a retraction, rephrasing his previous statement to be more accurate. (By the way, media publish erroneous statements, misquotes and completely inaccurate information on a regular basis, so an inexact statement is nothing extraordinary.) Kurtz later accepted a job as a media critic at Fox News.⁶⁰

Others have experienced the wrath of the media and gay activists if they make a verbal faux pas or publicly state they oppose gay marriage. The NBA fined Indiana Pacers center Roy Hibbert $75,000 for using the term "no homo" during a June 1, 2013 postgame news conference. Anyone familiar with urban vernacular knows that "no homo" is hardly a pejorative. It is an offhand term used when one person of the same gender gives the other a compliment about his or her physical appearance that might be perceived as a sexual advance.

For example, if a woman compliments another female on her well-toned physique, she might say "no homo" to indicate that her compliment is not based on a sexual attraction. It is in no way a slur against homosexuals. Yet, Hibbert's comment was labeled "homophobic" by the media and the NBA. He had to not only pay the fine but issue a public mea culpa.⁶¹

The media's approach of rewards for proponents of gay marriage and punishments for those in opposition will continue to intensify in the months and years ahead. Particularly in the political and entertainment arenas, media will make it more and more difficult for those who believe that marriage is between and man and a woman to express their opinions without paying a steep price.

CHAPTER 4
STICKS AND STONES MAY BREAK MY BONES...

Gay activists are extremely particular about the words people use to describe them and are very sensitive to any negative language that may be used against them. They have a long list of terms and descriptions which are off limits, including, but not limited to, "fag," "faggot," "homo," "dike," and "pervert," and rail against their orientation being associated in any way with pedophilia or bestiality. In addition, if a Christian says that homosexuality is a sin (which it clearly is, according to the Bible), gay activists respond as if they have been spat upon.

Yet, gay activists hurl some of the most vicious pejoratives at those who disagree with them, and they are aided by media representatives who often join in the fray. Over the past two decades, the name-calling has become more and more venomous. In the words of Ryan T. Anderson, a fellow with the Heritage Foundation, "They've sent a clear message: If you stand up for marriage, we will, with the help of our friends in the media, demonize and marginalize you."[62]

Who could have ever predicted that uttering the words, "I believe marriage is between a man and a woman," would become the metaphorical equivalent of spitting in one's face? What was once considered the accepted standard of American marriage relationships is now, somehow, passé.

I have yet to hear a member of the media criticize or castigate gay activists for their name calling. In other words, the media's thunderous silence connotes consent. But media also join in the fray by using complimentary terms for those who agree with gay marriage, and negative, critical ones for those who oppose it.

When Miss California, Carrie Prejean, was reportedly denied the Miss U.S.A. crown in the 2009 pageant because she honestly answered a direct question about gay marriage, indicating that she believed marriage should be between a man and a woman, she was verbally attacked via the media the following day by one of the judges. Perez Hilton, one of the pageant's judges who is himself gay, called Prejean a "dumb bitch" for her support of traditional marriage. Media's reaction: total silence.

Many reporters and commentators automatically label anyone who is opposed to gay marriage as "homophobic" or suffering from "homophobia." The use of this term, inappropriately and without evidence, paints everyone who opposes gay marriage with a broad brush, accusing them of an irrational fear of gay individuals. Frank Rich of the *New York Times* wrote a column in 2009 in which he described those against gay marriage as "spreading the poisons of bigotry and fear." Legal analyst Jeffrey Toobin used the term "bigotry" as well in his April 1, 2013 article in *The New Yorker* about how conservative Supreme Court justices treat the issue of gay marriage.[63]

I have personally been a direct target of gay activists' name-calling when I wrote a series of widely-published commentaries on gay marriage in 2009. After my op-eds were published, I was called everything but a child of God by gay activists, including an anti-gay bigot, a right-wing nut, a cow, a sow, a liar, a supremacist, an opportunist, ignorant, uneducated, filled with hate, backwards, and, of course, the "b" word. One gay Website added me to its "enemies list" with my photo included, and encouraged its cohorts to picket my office and bombard me with negative e-mails and harassing phone calls, all for merely exercising my right to free speech.

And the volume and asperity of the invectives is ever increasing. On May 12, 2012, Georgetown University professor and author, Michael Eric Dyson, was a substitute host for Ed Shultz, whose MSNBC program is titled "The Ed Show." The theme of the program was President Obama's statement in support of gay marriage, how the national polls had changed, and why black pastors should become more open to accepting marriage between same-sex partners.

"Black leaders of faith should not make the mistake of using the Bible to suppress the rights of the LGBT community, just as the Bible was used to suppress the rights of African Americans," said Dyson. "Throughout our nation's history, again and again, the Bible was cited to justify slavery and discrimination and laws against interracial marriage." He goes on to ask the question: "Do we want to become sexual rednecks?"

Clearly, Dyson has little respect for individuals who disagree with his opinion regarding gay marriage and does not believe they should be afforded even a basic level of personal respect. And Dyson is not alone as there doesn't seem to be a limit regarding the verbal abuse that can be used against someone who does not support gay marriage, especially those who oppose it on religious grounds.

Dyson fails to mention that the Bible neither encourages nor condones slavery, nor does it include any commandments against interracial marriage. Prior to the end of the Civil War, racists actually were able to misquote and misinterpret scripture because it was illegal for blacks to read; thus, they had no way of verifying these statements. For the next hundred years, blacks were allowed to learn to read, but the numbers who were truly literate were relatively small. Today, the prohibition and limits against reading no longer exist for black people, who can now read the Bible for themselves. And the Bible is clear and unequivocal regarding homosexuality in both the Old and New Testaments.

With Dyson's penchant for using rhymes and hip-hop language for the nonsensical diatribes in which he often engages, it can sometimes be difficult to follow his arguments or his line of reasoning. But his assessment during the program seemed to be that African Americans should be happy that gay activists, who have never genuinely been our political allies, have hijacked our history, using it as a stepping stone to both neutralize opposition and further their cause.

As stated in Chapter 1, when African Americans experience major acts of public injustice or humiliation, such as Trayvon Martin's murder in Florida, or the on-air insult to black female college basketball players by radio talk show host Don Imus, gay groups are nowhere to be found (unless they are, of course, headed by blacks). Blacks are left on our own to march, protest and denounce these injustices. Gay activists do not seem to want to have anything to do with African Americans, except to "pimp" our history for their own ends.

Dyson does not appear to direct the same vitriol toward believers of other religions who do not support homosexuality or gay marriage. The fact is that all of the world's major religions, including Islam and Orthodox Judaism, have prohibitions against homosexuality. Even religions with smaller numbers of adherents in the U.S., such as Buddhists and Mormons, do not endorse gay marriage.[64] And in most African nations that have large Muslim populations, the punishments for engaging in homosexual behavior can be quite severe.

During President Obama's trip to Africa in June 2013, he discovered that his personal support for gay marriage is not necessarily transferrable to foreign nations. When Obama visited Senegal, he urged the Senegalese people to make sure their government does not discriminate against gays. Obama was resoundingly rebuffed by Senegal's leader, President Macky Sall, as well as by its citizens and media. Senegal is one of 39

African countries that criminalize "consensual same-sex conduct," according to a report by Amnesty International.[65]

I want to make it perfectly clear that I do not condone the criminalization of homosexual activities. Rather, I'm pointing out Dyson's double standard of directing harsh criticism at Christians for merely stating what the Bible teaches about sexual immorality, including homosexuality, while failing to criticize Muslims or Orthodox Jews.

But Dyson has lots of company in terms of insults directed at individuals, including people of faith, who believe marriage should only be between a man and a woman. MSNBC's Chris Matthews, for example, described anyone who is against gay marriage as "crazy," during his April 9, 2013 broadcast.

Visit any news website, YouTube video or opinion piece published online that opposes gay marriage and read the comments from gay activists. The name-calling will be done in rapid fashion and in a highly personalized way. The term "homophobic" is, of course, commonly used. But the attacks tend to be extremely personal in nature. Here are just a few of the descriptions gay activists use for those who oppose gay marriage: stupid, liar, shallow, Neanderthal, hate-filled, backwards, and uneducated.

On some websites, it almost seems as though a committee of gay activists has been charged with the assignment of posting opposing comments on any site that is critical of gay marriage initiatives proposed around the country. A handful of posts under the same user names tend to repeatedly show up among the comments on each website, making the prospect of an assigned committee seem plausible.

Labeled as a "Hate Group"

The Southern Poverty Law Center (SPLC) has taken the name-calling a step further by labeling organizations that believe in and promote traditional marriage as "hate groups." Media representatives have repeated these claims, specifically regarding the Family Research Council, Traditional Values Coalition, American Family Association and the National Organization for Marriage. This label places these groups on par with organizations that have committed murder, overt acts of violence and racial terrorism, such as the Ku Klux Klan, Skinheads and White Aryan Resistance.

"The Southern Poverty Law Center (SPLC) was once a laudable civil rights organization that sued racists and violent extremists," writes Mark Hemingway in *The Weekly Standard*. "Now it regularly demonizes anyone who runs afoul of its knee-jerk liberal politics, and despite this it is still regularly cited by the media as a 'nonpartisan' watchdog."[66]

The SPLC website includes the following disclaimer regarding the hate groups it lists: "Listing here does not imply a group advocates or engages in violence or other criminal activity." Yet, when the Center lumps all groups together with those who have committed acts of violence, it does a disservice to the public as well as to groups whose primary infraction seems to be a difference of opinion with the Center on the issues of gay marriage and homosexuality. And it is unclear how an organization's name is removed from the list without rejecting its core beliefs.

If gay activists and their allies would like to be treated with respect, they should first respect others. Name-calling directed at those who oppose gay marriage is an intimidation tactic which may appear to be successful in the short-term, but in the long-term may fuel a backlash. A difference of opinion does not give gay activists the automatic right to be rude.

CHAPTER 5
PREVARICATION AND MENDACITY

One of the common techniques that members of the media use to expose dishonesty on the part of politicians and other public figures is to catch them red-handed when they plagiarize written documents, reverse political positions (also known as "flip-flopping"), make misstatements, or tell falsehoods. Media achieve this by playing video footage, soundbites or audiotapes from the past that contradict what the individual is presently saying.

Many politicians and others have had major career setbacks as a result of media using this technique, including sitting Vice President Joseph Biden. During the 1988 presidential campaign, Biden was caught plagiarizing portions of a British Labor leader's speech. Republican presidential nominee Mitt Romney also experienced a major campaign hiccup when media obtained the video recording of him denigrating the 47 percent of Americans who receive some sort of federal government benefits. But when gay activists are involved, media seem to be either disinterested in correcting their obvious errors and misstatements, or they are complicit in allowing these statements to go completely unchallenged.

The commonly used adage, "The first casualty of war is the truth," was first coined by U.S. Senator Hiram Warren Johnson in 1918.[67] Gay activists are, indeed, waging a guerilla war against those who oppose gay marriage, unbeknownst to most public observers. And, with the tacit support of the mainstream media, they have successfully promoted at least three themes at various times within the political and cultural zeitgeist which are completely untrue.

Misstatement #1: Ten Percent of the U.S. Population Is Homosexual

Gay activists have been making this declaration for at least two decades, with no empirical evidence whatsoever to validate these numbers. Members of the media themselves have repeated this false claim, requiring no substantiation and actually refusing to use their own data as well as common sense. To believe this claim, one has to fully accept the idea that one out of every ten individuals is homosexual and that, in any random group of one hundred people, ten of them will be gay. This is simply untrue.

As a contrasting example, 10 percent of the population is left-handed. One can actually survey any random group of ten individuals and at least one of them will have what's known as a South paw.

If members of the media wanted proof of the actual numbers of gay individuals, they have had several opportunities to validate these figures, including data they themselves have collected. For example, *The New York Times* published exit polls after each presidential election in 2004 and 2008 where they asked the sexual orientation of the voters. In both election cycles, 2 percent of the respondents said they were gay. And, in a Gallup poll released in October 2012, 3.4 percent of respondents said they were gay, which closely mirrors the *New York Times* data.

A similar percentage, 3.5, was revealed in a study by UCLA's Williams Institute, a think tank dedicated to conducting rigorous, independent research on sexual orientation and gender identity law and public policy.[68] An NBC News/*Wall Street Journal* poll conducted in April 2013 also showed that 3 percent of the population identifies as gay or lesbian.[69] Yet, I could not find evidence that even one media representative requested that gay groups correct this misinformation, nor have the media outlets published any stories or articles comparing the existing empirical data to the years of false claims made by gay organizations and their leaders.

Gay activists argue that the polls are not accurately capturing the size of the gay population, and that there are many homosexuals who are still "in the closet." However, that argument does not hold water for several reasons:

- The polls are blind surveys and respondents remain anonymous. Since there is no public pronouncement, there is no fear of being "outed."
- The percentages for all other ethnicities, races and the two genders are all deemed to be accurate. Why is it that other groups don't challenge their population estimates when presented as a result of blind surveys?

- In the *USA Today*/Gallup poll survey of respondents who identified themselves as lesbian, gay, bisexual or transgender, three out of four say they are generally open with others about their sexual orientation. More than nine of ten say people in their community have become more accepting in recent years.[70] Gay activists can't have it both ways. If the vast majority of LGBT individuals say they are "generally open," they certainly would not try to go into hiding to respond to a blind survey.

The fact that LGBT individuals have prominent roles in popular culture makes it appear that their numbers are greater than they actually are. The number of prominent gay television personalities actually far outnumbers those for Hispanics, who represent a much larger segment of the population.

The list of gay TV celebrities and influential media representatives is a long one, and includes the following individuals, who have all publicly declared their homosexuality. They are all in strategic and powerful positions within the industry.

Name	Network/Media Outlet – Position
Ellen DeGeneres	NBC - Talk show host
Sam Champion	ABC/Good Morning America - Host
Rachel Maddow	MSNBC - News anchor
Thomas Roberts	MSNBC - News anchor

Perez Hilton	Shut Up! Cartoons - TV personality
Anderson Cooper	CNN - News anchor
Don Lemon	CNN - News anchor
Suze Orman	CNN - TV host
Jann Wenner	US Weekly/Rolling Stone-Publisher
Kevin McClatchy	McClatchy Company - Founder
Harvey Levin	TMZ - Producer and founder
David Geffen	DreamWorks - Co-founder
Matt Drudge	Drudge Report - Founder/editor
Martha Nelson	*Time* magazine - Editor-in-chief
Andy Cohen	Bravo TV - TV executive/host
Chris Hughes	*The New Republic* - Editor-in-chief
Shepard Smith	Fox News - News anchor

In addition, gay characters play prominent roles in TV programs like Fox's "Glee" and "Family Guy," ABC's "Scandal" and "Modern Family," NBC's "The New Normal" (cancelled in 2013) and TNT's "Southland," to name a few. In actuality, empirical data shows that although gays represent a small segment of the American population, their access to the media provides them with a very loud megaphone.

The perception that homosexuals are 10 percent of the population, as opposed to 3 percent, also may affect the response to public pressure regarding gay marriage. The media's portrayal that gays are a large segment of the populace leads people to believe that, when presented with the option to support or oppose gay marriage, they must acquiesce in its support.

The concept of how Hollywood has helped the media to persuade the public will be discussed in more detail in Chapter 13.

Misstatement #2: "We're not interested in marriage."

About fifteen years ago, gay activists like Elizabeth Birch, then executive director of the Human Rights Campaign, the nation's largest LGBT organization, claimed they had no interest in pursuing gay marriage. "We don't want marriage," said Birch, when interviewed on television news programs in the mid-1990s. Birch is an attorney who also chaired the board of directors of the National Gay and Lesbian Task Force from 1992 to 1994.[71]

Gay activists asserted that all they wanted was equal protection under the law, hospital visitation rights and the right to transfer property in the event of a death. They said that civil unions would provide them with these protections, and these were measures that the majority of Americans, including myself, supported. At that time, Birch was the most prominent national spokesperson in the LGBT community.

At the same time Birch made this public pronouncement, gay activists were working on getting future marriage legislation passed in the states where they felt they had the best chances of success. This surreptitious action makes it obvious that marriage was the intention of LGBT activists all along, but they knew that, in the 1990s, this pursuit would alienate most voters. So they decided to bide their time and quietly pursue this goal, adopting an incremental approach.

The media footage of Birch's statements is certainly catalogued, since all major media outlets retain recordings of their broadcasts for decades. But for some reason, members of the media have ignored the existence of this archived material and have kept this sound bite in a metaphorical locked vault.

Misstatement #3: "We're not going to force churches to marry us."

This is the misstatement *du jour,* and the one which will present the greatest number of challenges in coming years for those who oppose gay marriage on religious grounds. In making this statement, gay activists are being particularly disingenuous because, while they may not actually sue churches to force religious leaders to perform gay weddings, they are waging a campaign of unbridled aggression against Christians individually, Christian business owners, and Christian-based organizations.

In a recent survey by the Pew Research Center, the religious basis for opposition to homosexuality was one of the primary reasons respondents gave for saying it should be discouraged by society. By far the most frequently cited factors -- mentioned by roughly half (52 percent) of those who say homosexuality should be discouraged -- were moral objections to homosexuality: that it conflicts with religious beliefs, or that it goes against the Bible.[72]

President Obama, in an attempt to set the minds of religious leaders at ease following the June 2013 Supreme Court ruling, essentially repeated the mantra advanced by gay activists: "How religious institutions define and consecrate marriage has always been up to those institutions. Nothing about this decision – which applies only to civil marriages – changes that."[73]

Since polls show that most of the opposition to gay marriage is based on religious convictions, gay activists have also attempted to allay the fears of church-goers by making the above statement and ones similar to it. And they began making this declaration several years ago.

Perez Hilton, a gay blogger and television personality, made a comparable statement during an April 21, 2009 interview on CNN's "Larry King Live," when he said that gay groups don't want to force churches to endorse or perform gay marriages. More recently, during an MSNBC interview in March 2013, gay activist Aisha Moodie-Mills, who is an analyst with the Center For American Progress, said, "We won't ask your clergy to marry us."

In an April 3, 2013 interview with Fred Luter, president of the Southern Baptist Convention, CNN's Anderson Cooper told Luter, "Churches would not be forced to marry [gay] people."

Yet, gay activists are engaging in a clandestine guerilla campaign to attack churches and people of faith on an individual basis, exacting a proverbial pound of flesh for those who choose not to compromise their religious beliefs for political expediency. For at least a decade, they have been taking legal action against churches that won't allow them to use their facilities for their "wedding" ceremonies, and against individual entrepreneurs who oppose gay marriage on religious grounds. Rather than attack organized churches and denominations head on -- an approach which would elicit strong resistance -- gay activists have targeted the low-hanging fruit of religious institutions and Christian entrepreneurs, small business owners of faith whose religious beliefs play a role in their family-owned enterprises.

Following are a few examples: In New York, the Albert Einstein College of Medicine at Yeshiva University, an orthodox Jewish institution, refused to allow same-sex couples to live in married student housing. In 2001, the New York State Supreme Court forced them to do so.

In Massachusetts, Catholic Charities were ordered to accept homosexual couples in their adoption service or close down. They chose to shut down this service.

A Methodist church in New Jersey was sued by a gay couple who wanted to use one of the church's facilities for a wedding ceremony. The church declined the building's use, but the couple filed a discrimination complaint with the state's civil rights division and the church lost its tax exempt status.

The challenge to the Methodist church's tax exempt status was done on the grounds that the building used was open to the public. It appears that gay organizations have found the Achilles heel of the Christian church: Since a major tenet of the Christian faith is that the church's doors are open to the public to bring people to Christ, virtually any church-owned building or property can be deemed a "public facility."

Churches regularly have youth rallies, barbecues, picnics, carnivals, concerts, etc., on their grounds to attract non-members and non-believers. They also erect buildings that are used for community centers, food pantries and homeless shelters that are not used for religious services, but which the churches actually own. This means that all churches are vulnerable to legal challenges from gay organizations.

Photographer in New Mexico

Subsequent to the legalization of gay marriage in several states, the attacks on Christian entrepreneurs have intensified. In August 2013, the New Mexico Supreme Court upheld the lower-court's ruling that forced, Elane Huguenin, a Christian photographer, to perform photo shoots at homosexual commitment ceremonies and other similar events. The court rejected the argument of the devout Christian owners who said they had a free speech and religious right not to shoot the ceremony.[74]

Although gay marriage is not legal in New Mexico, under the state's Human Rights Act, it's unlawful for a public accommodation to refuse to offer its services to someone because of the person's sexual orientation. The same law also prohibits discrimination on the basis of race, religion, color, national origin, ancestry and gender.[75]

The state body found that the Albuquerque-based company, Elane Photography, run by Huguenin and her husband, Jon, engaged in sexual orientation discrimination and ordered them to pay thousands of dollars in attorneys' fees. Although the plaintiff, Vanessa Willock, waived the attorneys' fees, the Huguenins were forced to hire their own attorney to defend their case. The ACLU, whose executive director, Anthony D. Romero, is gay, filed a brief in support of Willock.[76]

The New Mexico Supreme Court concluded: "When Elane Photography refused to photograph a same-sex commitment ceremony, it violated the NMHRA [New Mexico Human Rights Act] in the same way as if it had refused to photograph a wedding between people of different races." In other words, the justices equated race with homosexuality.[77]

Cake Shop Owner in Lakewood, Colo.

In Lakewood, Colo., a gay couple, Charlie Craig and David Mullins, filed a discrimination complaint against Jack Phillips, a cake shop owner who declined to create a cake for the couple's October wedding due to his religious beliefs. Although gay marriage is not legal in the state, Colorado law says it is illegal to discriminate based on sexual orientation in employment and housing. But the law is less than clear about commerce. Meanwhile, Phillips will likely be forced to retain an attorney to defend against the complaint.[78]

Vermont Bed and Breakfast

In August 2012, the owners of a Vermont Bed and Breakfast, Wildflower Inn, agreed to pay $10,000 in fines and another $20,000 in settlement funds surrounding same-sex civil union ceremonies held on their property. In 2000, then Governor Howard Dean signed a bill into law that would grant homosexuals "the same benefits and protections afforded by Vermont law to married opposite-sex couples." Wildflower Inn, however, had no requests for same-sex ceremonies until five years later when a lesbian couple asked the facility to host their service.

Jim and Mary O'Reilly, who own the Inn, told the couple that they would comply with the law by allowing the use of their facilities, but made clear that they objected to homosexual "marriage" because it was a violation of their religious beliefs. The couple was offended at the O'Reilly's response and filed a complaint with the Vermont Human Rights Commission, who stated that the O'Reillys had done nothing wrong by simply expressing their disagreement.

But in later years the O'Reillys hired a wedding coordinator to handle all ceremonies. In 2010, a lesbian couple inquired about having a wedding on the property and the coordinator responded by saying that facility did not accommodate homosexuals. The couple, with the help of the American Civil Liberties Union (ACLU), sued and the O'Reillys were forced to pay the fine.

T-Shirt Company in Lexington, Ky.

In November 2012, the Lexington-Fayette (Ky.) Urban County Human Rights Commission claimed that a local t-shirt company, Hands On Originals, violated a local ordinance based on sexual orientation. The company's owner, Blaine Adamson, refused to print t-shirts for the Gay and Lesbian Services Organization (GLSO) because he disagreed with the "gay pride" message the group wanted printed on the shirts. "If there's a specific message that conflicts with my convictions, then I can't promote that," said Adamson, in a video message.[79]

Adamson offered to direct GLSO to another business that could produce the shirts for the same price. Instead, GLSO filed a complaint and the company was cited for violating a local public accommodation ordinance mandating services not be denied based on sexual orientation. In its complaint, GLSO stated, "We aren't seeking monetary damages, we just want to raise awareness that this type of discrimination is occurring in Lexington."

In its response, Hands on Originals listed a number of customers whose t-shirt orders were declined because the messages conflicted with the owners' religious and moral convictions, including a shirt that read "Cummingtonite?" for a college club, and a shirt with a picture of Jesus walking on water next to a pirate ship. But the commission still ruled in favor of GLSO.

Gay activists argue that they have an "orientation," or attraction, for people of the same gender, in the same way a heterosexual has an "orientation" to be attracted to the opposite gender. Using that line of reasoning, Hands on Originals' initial infraction was that the company "discriminated" against the college club who wanted "Cummingtonite?" printed on their t-shirts. Perhaps the college club should file a claim under the same statute to test the veracity of the law.

Florist in Richland, Wash.

In April 2013, a Richland, Wash., florist, Barronelle Stutzman, owner of Arlene's Flowers, was sued for refusing to provide flowers for a gay wedding ceremony.[80] Stutzman said she adheres to the Biblical belief that marriage is "between a man and a woman." Gay marriage became legal in the state of Washington in November 2012.

The customers, Robert Ingersoll and Curt Freed, two gay men who had been long-time customers of Stutzman, could have purchased flowers from any number of florists in the area. Yet they chose to sue instead, an action clearly meant to intimidate other entrepreneurs who may not support gay marriage on religious grounds.

Before filing the lawsuit, Ingersoll and Freed's lawyers, working with the ACLU, sent a letter to Stutzman saying she had two options: (1) Either vow to never again discriminate in her services for gay people, write an apology letter to be published in the Tri-City Herald (the local daily newspaper), and contribute $5,000 to a local LGBT youth center, or (2) She would be sued for violating the Washington State Civil Rights Act.

The demand from the gay men's lawyers is clearly an act of extortion or financial terrorism. Why are the national media not bringing this threat to the public's attention?

The attacks on Stutzman by gay activists and their allies have been extreme. "It blew way out of proportion," Stutzman explained. "I've had hate mail. I've had people that want to burn my building. I've had people that will never shop here again and [vow to] tell all their friends."

Gortz Haus in Grimes, Iowa

A wedding venue in Grimes, Iowa, owned by Dick and Betty Odgaard declined to host a gay wedding in August 2013. Betty Odgaard is a Mennonite and said the decision was based on her religious beliefs. "We want to honor that. We want people to know that is our stand that comes from our faith, our convictions. I think we should just stand by that no matter what," she said. The Odgaards began receiving hate mail after taking their public stance.[81]

Donna Red Wing, executive director of One Iowa — which advocates for rights for same-sex couples — cried foul. Wing said that as a public venue, Gortz Haus is not protected under Iowa civil rights rules to deny services based on sexual orientation. Since the Iowa Supreme Court case Varnum v. Brien in 2009, Iowa has legally recognized same-sex marriage, but religious institutions are not required to recognize or perform such marriages. However, those protections do not extend to entrepreneurs whose faith intersects with their business pursuits.[82]

In every single one of the above instances, the gay couples or individuals could have easily taken their business elsewhere. The fact that the owners stated their religious beliefs up front as a reason for not promoting gay unions or homosexuality should be protected by the U.S. Constitution under religious freedom. It appears that gay activists specifically targeted the facilities *because* of their religious beliefs, to exact punishment and eventually put them out of business.

Declining to accept a new job order or take on a new client is something businesses do on a regular basis. A business can refuse to take an order or accept new business for any number of reasons:

- The job is too large for the business' capacity;
- The owner does not have experience with that type of work;
- The assignment is in a part of town that owner finds unfamiliar;

- The staff members with expertise in that area are already committed to other projects;
- The job would be too costly and the owner would lose money, rather than make a profit; or
- After checking client references, the business owner decides that he is not confident in the client's ability to pay for the job.

In fact, a business owner can make the determination to decline a new assignment for any reason he or she chooses, or for no reason at all. An entrepreneur doesn't have to do business with everyone who inquires. In fact, a business owner would not ordinarily know the sexual orientation of a gay or lesbian client, unless they make an issue of it or made it a condition for taking the job. After all, very few LGBT individuals walk around with t-shirts on that read, "I Am Gay."

Minnesota Same-Sex Marriage Law

On May 14, 2013, Minnesota Governor Mark Dayton signed into law a bill legalizing same-sex marriages in the state. While the law provides specific exemptions for religious entities from taking part in the solemnization of same-sex marriages, it does not exempt individuals, businesses, nonprofits or the secular business activities of religious entities from non-discrimination laws based on religious beliefs regarding same-sex marriage. Therefore, a business that provides wedding services such as cake decorating, wedding planning or catering services may not deny services to a same-sex couple who is planning a wedding based on their sexual orientation. In other words, the religious exemption in the Minnesota law is written so narrowly that it has no teeth whatsoever.[83]

And gay marriage does not have to be legalized in a state for a business or organization to be sued by gay activists. Passing an ordinance which includes sexual orientation among "protected" minorities empowers gay groups to target Christian-based entrepreneurs for lawsuits and harassment.

Churches and Christian-Based Organizations in California Are Targeted

After the Supreme Court ruled that opponents of gay marriage did not have standing to argue their case against California's legalization of nuptials for same-sex couples, the California Supreme Court lifted the ban in July 2013. This ruling gave gay activists in the state a green light to undertake aggressive action against Christians and churches across the state and they've hit the ground running.

According to sources in attendance at a minister's conference held in Los Angeles in August 2013, gay groups have begun sending questionnaires to churches asking them if they perform gay weddings. If the church answers "no," its pastor and parishioners are targeted for lawsuits.

In response to this threat on religious freedom, churches across the nation are moving to protect themselves against potential lawsuits from same-sex couples. Some churches are changing their bylaws to reflect their view that the Bible allows only marriage between one man and one woman.[84]

"I thought marriage was always between one man and one woman, but the Supreme Court in a 5-4 decision said no," said

Gregory S. Erwin, an attorney for the Louisiana Baptist Convention, an association of Southern Baptist churches and one of several groups advising churches to change their bylaws. "I think it's better to be prepared because the law is changing. America is changing."

In August 2013, the California Assembly considered a vote on a controversial bill by gay Democratic State Senator Ricardo Lara that would end state tax exemptions for the Boy Scouts of America and other youth groups if their membership policies discriminate based on sexual orientation. The bill, Senate Bill 323, is known as the Youth Equality Act (another example of gay activists' use of the word "equality" in their efforts to force individuals and groups to sanction homosexuality), and also names organizations such as Little League, Girl Scouts, Young Men's Christian Association (YMCA), 4-H Clubs, Special Olympics, Inc., American Youth Soccer Organization and Pop Warner football. Several of these organizations are Christian-based.[85]

Organizations established for children and youth should not be put in the position of screening their potential or existing members based on any sexual identity issues, including so-called orientation. Making inquiries on this basis is inappropriate, intrusive and violates the right to privacy.

These groups are established to develop wholesome activities for children, not to encourage or even acknowledge issues of a sexual nature. Their focus is to teach athletic skills, science, health, or community service, not to evaluate or address a child's sexual identity. Leaders of these groups are ill-equipped to handle the challenges arising from sanctioning homosexuality among the children within their midst.

Those concerns do not appear to matter to gay activists who are intent on mowing down anyone or any entity that stands in their way of elevating homosexuality to a protected status. Like a scythe that indiscriminately mows down a corn field, gay activists are relentless about punishing any individual, group, organization or institution that impedes their progress. In doing so, they place their own selfish interests above children's well-being.

Political Pressure in Houston

Although churches may not be required to perform gay wedding ceremonies in their buildings, religious leaders are not exempt from political pressure by politicians who support gay marriage. Leading up to the 2012 presidential election, Houston Mayor Anise Parker, who is gay, had members of her staff meet with black ministers in the city and asked them to stop preaching against homosexuality in their churches. This action was clearly a violation of church and state and sources said Parker met with strong resistance from the majority of those who were approached.

African Bishop Lost Job at Dartmouth

Most educational institutions should assume that a bishop of a Christian denomination would oppose gay marriage. But somehow Dartmouth College in New Hampshire assumed something different when they appointed Bishop James Tengatenga of Malawi to be dean of the school's William Jewett Tucker Foundation, which seeks to educate Dartmouth students "for lives of purpose and ethical leadership, rooted in service, spirituality and social justice."[86]

The appointment drew criticism after it was announced in July 2013 because of the bishop's leadership of an Anglican church in Africa that opposes gay rights. He served as diocesan bishop of Southern Malawi and chair of the Worldwide Anglican Communion's Anglican Consultative Council, a network of 44 churches.[87]

Not only does the Anglican Church oppose gay marriage but so do nearly all of the countries on the African continent, with the exception of South Africa. Dartmouth should have known the bishop's position on gay marriage in advance of the appointment. But pressure resulted after Andrew Longhi, a junior at Dartmouth, wrote a blog post on the *Huffington Post* website criticizing the appointment. Dartmouth President Philip Hanlon said the move came after much reflection and consultation with senior leaders at the college, adding that the institution's support of gay rights was "complete and unwavering."[88]

Federal Contracts for Religious Entities Are At Risk

To further financially cripple Christian-based companies and organizations, gay activists are encouraging President Obama to write an executive order barring federal contractors from discriminating on the basis of sexual orientation.[89] This will affect any religious entity that has a federal contract, and there are thousands of them.

Religious organizations have long competed for federal contracts to provide social services, like Head Start, after school, job training, youth mentoring, gang prevention and free lunch programs.[90] Funding for some programs is appropriated via Congressional earmarks. For example, an earmark provided $150,000 to help St. Jerome's Church in the Bronx, N.Y., build a community center; Fuller Theological Seminary in Pasadena, Calif., received $2 million to study gambling and juvenile violence.[91] In fiscal year 2011, the United States Conference of Catholic Bishops received $34 million in federal grants to provide social services to needy individuals.[92]

Earmarks have also helped finance new buildings on college campuses with a religious affiliation, including a fitness center at Malone College, a Christian liberal arts university in Canton, Ohio. And faith-based rescue missions and Catholic ministries often receive government grants and other funding for the work they do for the poor. It is a lot more cost effective to provide funding for religious organizations providing social services than it would be for the government to establish a new department or agency to fill the gaps in the already tattered social safety net.

Actions Taken In Other Countries Are Instructive

Countries that legalized gay marriage years ago present the best barometer for what we can expect in the United States. To the north of us in Canada, once gay marriage was legalized, it became illegal for religious leaders to say that homosexuality is a sin. If they do so, they are fined thousands of dollars by the government.

In February 2013, the Supreme Court of Canada ruled that Biblical speech opposing homosexual behavior, including in written form, is essentially a hate crime. Canadian William

Whatcott distributed flyers in 2001 and 2002 regarding the Bible's prohibitions against homosexuality and was ordered to pay $7,500 to two homosexuals who took offense to his flyers, as well as to pay the legal fees of the Human Rights Commission, which amounted to hundreds of thousands of dollars.[93]

Nelson Zavala, an evangelical preacher in Ecuador who ran for president in 2013 was sentenced after he was found guilty of violating the country's electoral code by speaking against homosexuality. Zavala was fined more than $3,000 and banned from running for office or being involved with any political party for one year because of a speech he gave where he stated he believes homosexual behavior is "immoral" and that it is a "severe deviation of conduct."[94]

Although gay marriage is not yet legal in Ecuador, the nation's 2008 Constitution enacted civil unions between two people without regard to gender, giving same-sex couples the same rights as legally married heterosexual couples except for the right to adopt.

In England, two gay dads are set to sue the church over its same-sex marriage opt out. The dads, Tony and Barrie Drewitt-Barlow, were joined in a civil partnership ceremony in 2006 and, together, have fathered five children through surrogate mothers. They are also the first British same-sex couple to be named on their children's birth certificates.[95]

Britain legalized gay marriage when the Queen gave her royal stamp of approval on July 17, 2013 but, apparently, that's not enough for the Barlows. "I want to go into my church and marry my husband," said Barrie, in an interview with the *Essex Chronicle*. "We need to convince the church that it is the right thing for our community for them to recognize us as practicing Christians."⁹⁶

Why Do Gay Activists Target Churches?

Although gay activists make false claims about not forcing churches to change their doctrine and policies, it is clear that their intent is to slowly chip away at the Christian church's foundations with regard to homosexuality. There are three major reasons why churches are being targeted.

First, individuals in the U.S. who are openly gay are much less likely than the general population to have a religious affiliation. According to a poll by the Pew Research Center, 48 percent of LGBT adults do not identify with a particular religion, versus 20 percent of the general public.⁹⁷ Members of the LGBT community are also three times as likely to be atheists as the general population, and 65 percent of gays and lesbians say they seldom or never attend religious services.⁹⁸

Second, individuals in the general population who are unaffiliated with a religion of any kind are more likely to favor gay marriage. Seventy-four percent of those who do not have a religious affiliation support gay marriage, versus much lower percentages for Catholics and Protestants, according to the Pew Research Center.⁹⁹

Third, and most importantly, religion represents the final obstacle to nationwide gay marriage and gay activists will wage an ongoing battle with the church and anyone with religious beliefs until their victory has been achieved. While support for gay marriage among the overall public may be at about 50 percent, it is lowest among white evangelical and black Protestants. Only 23 percent of white evangelical Protestants support gay marriage. The support among black Protestants is higher – 32 percent – but nowhere near the majority, and those percentages have remained steady for the past decade.[100]

Religious Exemptions Have No Teeth

Most of the states that have legalized gay marriage have also included a religious exemption in the legislation. With the insertion of these exemptions, the legislators were able to get religious leaders to support the measures. The wording differs from state to state.

In New York, which legalized gay marriage in 2011, Republicans insisted on the provision and not only wanted religious organizations and affiliated groups to be protected from lawsuits if they refused to provide their buildings or services for same-sex marriage ceremonies, but they also wanted to be spared any penalties by state government. New Hampshire and several other states, which also approved same-sex marriage bills, included similar protections.[101]

Religious leaders may have assumed that these exemptions would protect the flock and maintain the tenets of their faith. But the mistake well-meaning Christians so often make is believing that gay activists will act honorably regarding respect for religious tenets and institutions.

Instead, these exemptions are meaningless and carry little, if any, weight, for two reasons. One, gay activists made sure that the exemptions were carefully worded and narrowly focused to specifically exclude the attacks on individual religious freedoms that they knew they were about to wage.

The second reason is that gay activists have clearly demonstrated that they have no intention of abiding by these exemptions. The evidence lies in the fact that they have already begun waging legal challenges against any individuals or entities that, on religious grounds, refuse to sanction gay marriage by participating in same-sex weddings or gay-oriented activities. The American Civil Liberties Union (ACLU), whose executive director, Anthony D. Romero, is, coincidentally, gay, is leading the charge with these lawsuits, and they are being waged from coast to coast.[102]

Legal System No Longer Protects Religious Freedom

It appears that the system of jurisprudence is behind the curve when it comes to protecting the religious freedoms of individuals and entrepreneurs. In many cases, from the vantage point of the religious proprietor, the decision to accept a project for a gay cause is tantamount to the promotion of homosexuality. If the political system is not going to protect entrepreneurs who, on principal, refuse to promote homosexuality, then these business owners will need to become more savvy about the legal system or fight these folks all the way to the Supreme Court.

After all, the essence of Christianity is not the building or edifice where Christians worship. Jesus spoke to the people as they gathered at river banks, in open fields, in caves, on boats, and, yes, in temples. But it is the people who are the body of Christ and represent Christianity. When the faith of one Christian is attacked, essentially, the faith of all Christians is attacked.

Requiring Christians to promote or validate homosexuality is like asking an Orthodox Jew or a Muslim to eat pork. The government, according to our Constitution, does not have this right and the exercise of religion is protected in the First Amendment.

Until the courts start protecting Christians, as they should, business owners may need to use a different approach. When they are confronted with these types of situations where gay activists try to force them to promote homosexuality against their religious beliefs, they may need to exercise prudence and offer reasons other than religion for their decision. Kroger stores, for example, have a policy of not carrying authors' books if they are "too controversial." Controversy can manifest in many forms and is a subjective criterion. Kroger wisely uses its discretion in the decision-making process.

To be clear, Kroger's policy is not geared toward the homosexual community. The store simply prefers not to create headaches for itself by displaying any literature on its shelves which might result in a large swath of disgruntled customers. For example, the store will not approve an author's book whose subject matter is related to Child Protective Services cases. Nor will it allow books on its shelves that promote a particular religious denomination or sect, although the store does carry inspirational and general Christian books. Kroger has made a determination that controversy is simply not good for the grocery business.

Media Rarely Report Attacks on Religion by Gay Activists

This body of evidence, which is substantial, is something that, apparently, the media want to keep a secret, since they will rarely give nationwide exposure to these types of incidents. In order to even find out about them, one must conduct extensive personal research online. The news items are published in the local newspapers in the jurisdictions where the incidents occurred. But the national media ignore them and, without Christian media, they would go largely unreported beyond local boundaries.

It is obvious that gay activists intend to attack Christians from all sides and are using the courts and legislatures to accomplish this goal, despite their assertions to the contrary via the media. The church building may be spared, but Christians certainly will not.

CHAPTER 6
ENDORSING THE "BORN THAT WAY" MYTH

One of the first rules of journalism and commentary writing that one learns is to avoid expressing opinions in absolute terms. Describing people, situations and concepts with an "all or nothing" approach is considered a no-no and, when this faux pas is committed by journalists, an editor almost always corrects it before the article or opinion piece is released to the public.

Yet, the media allow gay activists to proclaim, without correcting them, that *everyone* who engages in homosexual behavior is "born that way." Activists are not challenged on the voracity of this claim and, instead, media join them in agreement. These activists offer no scientific proof and media do not require it. In fact, no proof exists because there is no gay gene. Instead individuals who are gay themselves will often utilize anecdotes and declarative statements like, "I was born this way," or "I felt differently from my earliest memory," as their proof.

The majority of media representatives have accepted this hypothesis, no questions asked. For example, on numerous occasions, MSNBC's Chris Matthews has said, "That's the way God made them," when referring to gays and lesbians, as if he has had a personal conversation with God and received a direct message to that effect. Matthews has also said, "My view is that we're all God's children," as if Christians disagree.

Matthews is Catholic and, thus, he should know that most Christians believe the Bible is the depository of God's word. The Bible clearly states, in both the Old and New Testaments, that homosexual acts are forbidden and should be avoided, and that all sex outside of marriage is a sin. It also says that God created male and female and that, when Adam was alone in the Garden of Eden, God made him a female companion (Eve).

Attempting to determine what God was thinking at the time of the Biblical creation of man is a risky proposition. But, one could hypothesize that, if God (or nature) wanted men to mate with each other for procreative purposes, He could have designed the male body so it could reproduce and, thus, females would be unnecessary. In other words, He could have created Adam and Steve, instead of Adam and Eve. Or God could have done the same thing with females. Obviously, that did not happen.

Others in the media seem to share Matthews' view, as I have rarely, if ever, heard anyone challenge this statement or even interview someone who disagrees. Media have eagerly joined in the promotion of that concept. Yet, the truth is much more complex.

The same way that computers, lap tops and smart phones are hard-wired with USB ports, human beings are hard-wired to be heterosexual. The human body is designed with a reproductive system which complements the opposite gender. That is how humans have procreated since the beginning of time and how the human species continues, generation after generation into infinity. Every human being who has ever walked the Earth has had a mother and a father in terms of the egg and sperm that were required to bring them into existence. The sexual attraction between males and females is what makes this miraculous system work.

Gay activists will often cite studies which supposedly provide proof of a genetic disposition toward homosexuality. The study referenced most often by gay advocates to support the "born that way" claim is the body of research conducted on twins. The most frequently cited one was released by the Pacific Center for Sex and Society.[103]

There are three aspects of the methodology which make the results of this and other studies questionable:

1) The participants were solicited from advertisements in gay publications, which means they not only were self-selected but also suggests that they were already predisposed to a particular point of view.

2) The fact that the twins were raised in the same household reinforces the likelihood of socialization playing a prominent role in their "orientation."

3) The sample sizes are too small to provide conclusive data.

Indeed, Jason Collins, the gay NBA player who was discussed in Chapter 3, has a twin brother who is not gay, which further debunks the theory of a genetic link of homosexuality between twins.

Then there are other studies which suggest that certain physical characteristics are more common in homosexuals than heterosexuals. Gay activists then take the giant leap that these characteristics are proof of a genetic connection. Here are some examples of supposed scientific proof:

- The hair whorl among some gay males is more likely to be counterclockwise than clockwise.[104]
- Gay men and straight women have an increased density of fingerprint ridges on the thumb and pinkie of the left hand.[105]
- The index fingers of most straight men are shorter than their ring fingers, and for most women they are the same length or longer. Gay men and lesbians tend to have reversed traits.[106]
- Gay men and lesbians have a 50 percent greater chance of being left-handed or ambidextrous than their straight counterparts.[107]

At best, these are random characteristics which are not present in even the majority of gay individuals. In fact, one would have much more evidence to reach a conclusion that black people are born with rhythm. Although the presence of rhythm is cultural, not genetic, the vast majority of black people appear to possess it. Yet, one cannot use the existence of rhythm to conclude it is, therefore, transmitted through the genes.

The random characteristics offered by gay activists are not proof of a genetic component at all. And with the small sample sizes of gay individuals who are not randomly selected, the results reflect a bias rather than hard data for which a definitive conclusion can be drawn.

For example, regarding the direction of the hair whorl as a characteristic, scientists found that the direction of the whorl can actually be subjective (two people can look at the same photograph and reach opposite conclusions about the whorl's direction); it is hard to see in people with long or curly hair, and could be seen in only 10 percent of black newborns.[108]

Further, one of the studies, by Dr. A. J. S. Klar in 2004, recorded the direction of hair whorls at a beach near Rehoboth Beach, Del., that is popular among gay men. Out of 272 men with single whorls, 29.8 percent had counterclockwise whorls. This was a higher proportion than the 9.1 percent counterclockwise he counted in 328 men from malls, stores and the beach at Atlantic City, most of whom were presumed to be straight. This result received widespread media coverage, particularly on gay websites.[109]

However, two more rigorous studies did not find a significant difference between gay and straight men in the proportion of counterclockwise whorls. One cannot credibly take a giant leap from Klar's findings and conclude that all gay men have a counterclockwise hair whorl, especially when, even using his non-random sample, only about one-quarter of the men possessed the whorl in the "gay" direction.[110]

At What Age Does One Discover Gayness?

Homosexuals say that, instead of being attracted to individuals of the opposite sex, they are sexually attracted to those of the same gender. In the case of bisexuals, they are attracted to those of either or both genders. Many say they have had this attraction as far back as they can remember and that, therefore, they were "born that way," or that it is an "orientation."

Interestingly, a poll of gay men and women conducted by the Pew Research Center in June 2013 seems to contradict the "born that way" concept. The pollsters asked the respondents at what age they first had an inkling that they were gay. The median age at which gay men said they had their first inkling was 10, and they knew for sure by 15. For women, the median age was considerably higher. The median age when the realization dawned on the lesbians surveyed was 13, and they were certain by 18. The median age when gay men first told someone was 18, and 21 for lesbians.[111] If sexual orientation is present at birth, then why does it take until puberty or adolescence before individuals realize it?

Again, no "gay gene" has been discovered and there is no conclusive scientific evidence that this is an inherent trait. Rather, a number of factors frequently seem to be major components of the life experiences of most homosexuals, particularly in childhood. This does not mean that everyone who has these traumatic experiences will become homosexuals. But it does mean that there is a strong correlation between the two.

Although most gay activists will claim that the individuals who experience these traumas and subsequently engage in homosexual behavior are exceptions to the rule, they are simply too numerous to ignore. But ignore them they must in order to perpetuate the concept of "orientation," rather than choice.

Some factors apply universally to both males and females, while others are gender-specific. We will first explore those that apply to both genders.

Childhood Molestation and Rape

The occurrence of childhood molestation and rape is a recurring theme in the life experiences of homosexuals who openly discuss their backgrounds. In fact, it is such a recurring theme that it must be acknowledged, unless gay activists believe that children who are molested deserve it because they were already predisposed to be homosexuals and, thus, were somehow attracted to their tormenters. Many of the boys and young men who have been molested by priests in the Catholic church later engage in homosexual behavior.

While letting these sexual predators off the hook, gay activists refuse to even acknowledge that such victims exist because their existence is proof that the so-called "gay gene" theory is flawed. Child psychologists agree that children who are sexually molested, whether at the hands of someone of the same sex or the opposite sex, are very likely to have sexual identity problems as adults. For boys, the abuse, particularly if the molester is male, can ignite those struggles into a sexual identity crisis. The issue is also difficult for male victims, experts say, because their bodies may have physiologically responded to the abuse.[112]

A number of openly gay writers have, in their memoirs, suggested that childhood sexual molestation might be the root cause of their resultant homosexuality. Roy Simmons, a former NFL player, wrote in his autobiography, *Out of Bounds: Coming Out of Sexual Abuse, Addiction and My Life of Lies in the NFL Closet*, that he was raped at age 10.

Gospel Artist Donnie McClurkin

Donnie McClurkin, an award-winning gospel artist, says he was 8 years old when he was raped by an uncle. McClurkin, whose 2001 memoir *Eternal Victim, Eternal Victor* detailed his childhood molestation, has since renounced his homosexual lifestyle, saying in a public testimony, "If it hadn't been for this Jesus, I would be homosexual to this day. But He [Jesus] is a deliverer."

Gay activists, however, have McClurkin in their crosshairs. In August 2013, McClurkin was uninvited from a MLK Memorial concert in Washington, D.C. It appeared that D.C. Mayor Vincent C. Gray heeded the demands of gay rights activists who wanted McClurkin dropped from the event marking the 50th anniversary of the March on Washington. The New Jersey-based pastor has previously shared his belief that God delivered him from the "sin of homosexuality" and that people with unwanted same-sex attractions can change.[113]

Regina Griggs, who heads the group known as Parents and Friends of Ex-Gays and Gays (PFOX), said that, with the exclusion of McClurkin, gay activists revealed just how intolerant they can be. "Supreme Court Justice Anthony Kennedy cited public 'animus' against gays as a reason to strike down part of the Defense of Marriage Act, yet gay rights groups promote hatred against former homosexuals," she said.

"Respecting the lives of people like Donnie, who have decided to change, and including them in the conversation, is part of building a tolerant society."[114]

Dr. Loren Due

Dr. Loren Due, a minister based in California, exposes his childhood nightmare of incest, molestation and rape at the hands of his biological father and brother in his memoir, *Teddy Bear: Stolen Innocence.* Due grew up in Southern California in a home where his father, who was a Pentecostal pastor, and his brother, who later became a Pentecostal pastor, molested and raped him beginning at the age of 4 or 5 years, while his mother worked three jobs to provide for the family's necessities.

"I became promiscuous at age 7 and started oral sex with girls," says Due. Although he received Christ at age 11 and was baptized, Due says, "My life was primarily bisexual with men and women. I was just a sexual animal."

After spending his teen years in a downward spiral of drugs, alcohol and homosexual and bisexual promiscuity, and a failed marriage at age 31, Due's life was later transformed by a renewed, rebirth experience. "In 1986, the Lord spoke to me and I gave it all up," he says. "He [God] let me know that I could lead a celibate life and sustain it."

Due met his wife during those years of celibacy and they have been married for more than 20 years. "It took a while to totally commit, but for the last 25 years, I've been serving the Lord."

The California native also counsels those seeking deliverance from homosexuality, and says that 80 percent of the people he counsels have a background that includes childhood molestation. "We minister the word of God and let them know that they have a choice."

When asked how his counseling method differs from reparative therapy, which was banned in the state of California in 2012 by Governor Jerry Brown, Due says, "The difference between what reparative therapy says and what I do is that we talk to people who want to talk to us, who are uncertain about what the Bible says about these issues of sexual behavior. We simply let them know what the Bible says and they make their choice."

Referring to the methods used by Exodus International, the reparative therapy group that closed the doors of its North American operation in June 2013, Due says, "Their idea was to brainwash somebody and bring them to a heterosexual lifestyle. Condemnation is the focus of reparative therapy. We offer love, rather than condemnation."

However, gay activists do not appear to distinguish among the methods or motives of those who offer counseling for deliverance from homosexuality. Any individual or organization that operates from the premise that change is possible is verbally attacked and becomes the subject of character assassination.

Yet, Due seems to be undaunted by the possibility of a negative response from gay activists. For those who say that they were born gay, Due has a message of redemption. "We are all born in sin," he says, "but there is miracle-working power in the Holy Spirit."

CNN Anchor Don Lemon

At least one member of the media has also had a similar experience with childhood molestation. CNN's Don Lemon admitted on live television in September 2010 that he was molested by a pedophile when he was a child. A few weeks later, Lemon also declared that he was openly gay.

Sexual Experimentation

Another major correlating factor regarding homosexuality is experimentation. Sexual experimentation among adolescents is commonplace and, even if it does occur with members of the same sex, it is more a function of childhood curiosity than sexual orientation. If teenagers are told that sexual experimentation with someone of the same gender is the equivalent of some sort of "orientation," they may accept that determination even though most would naturally adapt to a heterosexual existence once they matured.

Actress Anne Heche, another victim of childhood molestation by her biological father, provides a high-profile example of sexual experimentation. Heche dated men early in her adult life. In 1997, Heche publicly announced she was gay and that she was intimately involved with comedian Ellen DeGeneres. Three years later, she went back to dating men and, shortly thereafter, married Coley Laffoon, whom she divorced in 2007. Heche still dates men and gave birth in 2009 to a baby boy fathered by actor James Tupper. She has stated that, except for her relationship with DeGeneres, all of her other romantic relationships have been with men.[115]

Fashion designer Angela Bacskocky of Richmond, Va., who was a contestant on Season 12 of the Lifetime reality show "Project Runway," admitted to experimenting with a same-sex relationship after a failed marriage. "I tried being a lesbian for awhile," said Bacskocky on the season's opening program on July 18, 2013. "But it didn't work. I found out I wasn't."

Sexual experimentation occurs on a regular basis. But just because someone experiments with same-sex intimacy, this does not mean that person has an "orientation." It simply means they act on their curiosity.

Early Exposure to Pornography

In a public sermon about homosexuality that McClurkin delivered in 2009, he made this profound statement, "What enters into the eyes goes into the soul," referring to the exercise of watching pornography on the television or computer.

Apparently, that was the case for several teens with the Passion For Christ Movement who participated in an on-camera roundtable discussion about how they became involved with homosexuality, and identified early exposure to pornography as a gateway toward participating in same-sex relationships. A segment of the roundtable discussion among the teens affiliated with the Passion for Christ Movement can be viewed on YouTube here:
http://www.youtube.com/watch?v=YKOEEgsdUzQ

Many of these young people began watching pornography, either on the Internet or with friends, while in middle school. As teenagers, some went online to chat rooms and dating sites and engaged in one-time sexual encounters, threesomes and orgies.

Several said that they had to consume drugs or alcohol to relax their level of resistance. The media, with its 24/7 promotion of homosexuality, bisexuality and an "anything goes" attitude toward sex, fed their idea that what they were doing was the latest thing, even though many said their conscience told them otherwise. The MTV network was singled out as a channel which aggressively promotes both homosexuality and bisexuality.

Teenage Rebellion

When teenagers go through their rebellious stage, it is common for them to intentionally engage in behaviors in which they know their parents will not approve. Some teens smoke cigarettes or marijuana, some drink liquor, some get tattoos or wild hairstyles and, yes, some declare themselves to be homosexual. The teens know this declaration will likely shock and, in some cases, incense their parents and that is the intended goal. As with other rebellious behaviors teenagers adopt, some continue throughout adulthood while others do not.

Factors Prevalent Among Gay Males

The following additional correlating factors were cited among gay males and those who counsel them as having an influence on their sexual orientation.

- **Abusive or emotionally distant father/stepfather.** Although males are inherently aggressive, they still have a strong need for platonic, non-sexual male love which they usually receive from their fathers. When their fathers or stepfathers are emotionally cold or abusive, the desire for male love is still present in the child. He may subsequently seek this affection in the form of a homosexual relationship.

- **Incorrect gender assignment by mother,** coupled with the absence of a father's presence in the home. Some women have a strong desire to give birth to a female child and, when a male child is born instead, they will treat the child as though he was a girl. This includes wardrobe, hairstyles, peer groups and socialization.
- **Environment surrounded by feminine influences.** Boys who are in families where they are the only male sibling among many may adopt some of the feminine mannerisms and characteristics of their sisters.
- **Being labeled "soft" or a "punk" as an adolescent.** Male children exhibit varying degrees of masculinity and toughness. Some male children who are perceived as being weak or effeminate will be bullied and labeled as "punks" by their peers. In the same way that a female will begin to believe she is unattractive if she is constantly described as "ugly," a segment of this male group will respond to this bullying by internalizing the labeling and beginning to question their sexual orientation. Some will then act on this uncertainty by engaging in homosexual relationships.

Factors Prevalent Among Lesbian Females

The following additional correlating factors were cited among lesbian females and those who counsel them as having an influence on their sexual orientation.

- **No affirmation or reinforcement about their femininity; labeled "tomboy" at early age.** Some girls are never told that they are attractive and receive no reinforcement from a loving male figure. They are labeled "tomboys" because they like to participate in activities usually geared toward male children. As a result, they begin to present themselves with a masculine appearance (e.g., short hair, male clothing, no jewelry or makeup) and seek intimacy with accepting females.

    Janet Boynes, author of the book *Called Out: A Former Lesbian's Discovery of Freedom*, regarded herself as a tomboy during her childhood and describes those years this way: "I longed to be with and be like boys and men because I thought that they were stronger than women and didn't experience pain and suffering."[116]

    At age 13, Boynes was sexually abused by the father of one of her sisters and later began using drugs and alcohol. She eventually began living a lesbian lifestyle, moving from one relationship to the next. Finally, after 14 years living as a lesbian, she met a woman at a grocery store who invited her to church. She began to study God's word and gave up drugs and alcohol. For more than a decade, she has been free from homosexuality and has no regrets. "My story is proof that it doesn't matter how far you've gone, or what you've done, God still calls, and He calls in love."[117]

- **Bitterness about past failed relationships with men.** After experiencing one or more traumatic relationships with men where they have been heartbroken or abused, or both, some women will reject intimacy with men altogether. They will then seek intimacy with women, believing that these relationships are less likely to cause the same level of emotional trauma.

The series of online interviews with the young people in the group called the Passion For Christ Movement (www.p4cm.com), mentioned previously, is both enlightening and instructive. Their individual childhood experiences include most of the above-described factors. Members of this youth group were previously involved in homosexuality or bisexuality and say they have been delivered through the power of Jesus Christ.

During the interviews, they are very open about what led them down this road, without being graphic. Some of them were raised in homes where church attendance was expected, but most were not. Many of them say they were molested as children, some as early as 5 years old. The molestation opened the door to sexuality at a time when children should have all of their innocence intact. Exposure to pornography and sexual experimentation followed.

The members of P4CM say they each, individually, cried out to God to save them and give them a heart that sought what they believed was God's will for their lives. They were able to get support from the P4CM organization and have been able to stay free from homosexuality for several years.

A question that gay activists should answer is this: If people are molested as children, obviously through no fault of their own, and the molestation leads to feelings of same-gender attraction that they prefer to eliminate, why shouldn't they be provided the opportunity to do so? Or if they begin to have homosexual attractions as a result of experimentation or early exposure to pornography, doesn't that automatically negate a predisposition?

From my observation, gay activists dismiss and/or attempt to discredit any individuals who say they have been delivered from homosexuality. They will accuse them of lying, claiming that they are not really delivered but are fabricating their entire experience. However, just because these same gay activists believe it is not possible for *them*, does not mean it is impossible for *everyone*.

But there are thousands of gay and lesbian individuals who have successfully turned away from homosexuality because they made a decision to do so and sought assistance or support for their efforts. For many of these individuals, there was a religious or spiritual component to their transformation. Details about this transformation process will be discussed in the next chapter.

CHAPTER 7
ENDORSING THE "IF YOU'RE GAY, YOU CAN'T CHANGE" MYTH

Once the media collectively embrace the myth that all homosexuals are "born that way," a logical extension of that embrace is that they also believe and promote the concept that all homosexuals are gay for life with no possibility of change. Anyone who suggests otherwise is summarily denounced and any organization that has a mission to provide counseling to those who pursue change or deliverance is vilified and discredited, or worse.

To bolster their argument, gay activists emphasize the 1973 decision of the American Psychological Association (APA) to declassify homosexuality as a mental illness. Then they make the giant leap of concluding that, because of the APA's declassification, change is, therefore, impossible. The two are not mutually exclusive.

In addition, gay activists fail to mention that Dr. Nicholas Cummings, the former president of the APA who led the movement for declassification, has since changed his position and says that leaving the homosexual lifestyle is indeed a possibility. Cummings said, in an interview with psychologist Joseph Nicolosi, that 20 percent of the homosexuals who came to him to change did so. He also said that the APA has been taken over by "ultraliberals" beholden to the gay rights movement, has become more political than scientific, and that dissenting opinions regarding homosexuality are not allowed.[118]

Cummings admits that for those who wish to leave the gay lifestyle, the therapy can be challenging. "It's a difficult therapy," he said, "and it's not huge in terms of numbers, but yes we have seen success, and this is why the stance that 'you can never change'—Ronald Reagan said 'never say never'—it's absurd. All you have to do is find one exception and it knocks down the 'never.' But yes, I've experienced more than one exception."[119]

Exodus International North America

In June 2013, Exodus International, an organization whose mission was to assist homosexuals with overcoming same-sex attractions through scripture and prayer, announced it was shutting down its operations in the U.S. Alan Chambers, the group's president, issued an apology to any gays and lesbians who had been harmed by Exodus' practices, known as conversion therapy. Media immediately seized on Chambers' statements saying that the organization's demise proved that homosexuals cannot change under any circumstances.

When she hosted a CNN segment regarding the closing of Exodus International, the network's anchor, Suzanne Malveaux, questioned whether or not Chambers should have done more. "Is an apology good enough?" Malvaeux asked during a June 20, 2013, on-air discussion of the Exodus announcement. It was unclear what punishment Malveaux would have prescribed for

Chambers. Perhaps she felt that wearing a sack cloth and ashes or some other sort of public humiliation was in order.

During the segment, Eric Marrapodi, CNN Senior Producer and Belief Blog Co-Editor, claimed to speak for all Christians, stating that "Christians disavow the idea that homosexuality is a choice." He offered no evidence whatsoever of his claim and extensive polling on the views of Christians regarding whether or not they believe homosexuality is a choice has not been conducted. CNN's Belief Blog also includes the views of atheists, so the network is clearly approaching "belief" from a secular point of view.

The next day, MSNBC's Chris Matthews continued the discussion with a segment on his "Hardball" program labeled, "Pray Away the Gay?" During the segment, Matthews made the mistake so often made by those in the media who support gay marriage: He assumed that the failures of Exodus International equate with the failure of any and all efforts of this kind.

Wayne Besen, a gay man who is executive director of Truth Wins Out, said these efforts *always* fail, "then the victim is blamed for the failure." Besen added, "You cannot pray away the gay," and that the programs represent "an obstacle course of idiocy." On its website, Truth Wins Out describes itself as "a non-profit organization that fights anti-gay religious extremism."

During the same segment on "Hardball," Dr. Laura Berman, a sex psychotherapist, said emphatically, "Reparative therapy is based on the assumption that being gay is a choice, and it's *not* a choice," as if she can speak for every practicing homosexual in the entire world.

Although Exodus North America closed its doors, the organization still continues to operate in Latin America. In fact, following the closure of the entity's American component, the Latin American division's board of directors released a statement in July 2013 disavowing the declarations made by Chambers and other Exodus staffers in the U.S. In addition, the statement emphasized that the mission of Exodus Global Alliance would continue to be, "Proclaiming that for those who experience same-sex attraction or who are involved in homosexuality, it is possible through faith in Jesus Christ to have a life transformed by Him."[120]

However, there are thousands of individuals who have successfully converted from homosexuality to heterosexuality who Besen, Berman and others like them choose to ignore or summarily dismiss. Besides Exodus, there are a number of other ministries that work with homosexuals and have successfully assisted them with overcoming homosexual ideations and behavior.

- The Restored Hope Network includes the largest and oldest former Exodus "member ministries" (www.restoredhopenetwork.org).
- The Overcomers Network, formed in 2010, has a mission of utilizing small group units and annual events to work with those who have overcome homosexuality. Its website features a listing of churches that are "Ex-LGBT affirming," and that invite the "redeemed to come and fellowship in a righteous and holy environment." (www.overcomersnetwork.org)

- The Hope for Wholeness Network, a group of ministries that includes some former Exodus members, has formed in South Carolina. It exists so that those "who struggle with homosexuality find freedom to live in sexual and relational wholeness according to God's design." (www.hopeforwholeness.org)
- Parents and Friends of Ex-Gays (PFOX) supports families, advocates for the ex-gay community, and educates the public on sexual orientation. (www.pfox.org)
- Voice of the Voiceless (VOV) is an advocacy organization formed to combat negative stereotypes and defend the rights of former homosexuals, individuals with unwanted same-sex attractions, and their families. VOV celebrated its first Ex-Gay Awareness Month in September 2013. (www.voiceofthevoiceless.info)

Political Response to Reparative Therapy

The political response of gay activists to reparative therapy has been to encourage state legislatures to ban the practice. In 2012, California became the first state to implement this ban. In August 2013, New Jersey Governor Chris Christie signed a bill banning reparative therapy for minors. Two other states — Massachusetts and New York — have introduced similar bans in their state legislatures in 2013.[121]

The Southern Poverty Law Center (SPLC) has filed a consumer fraud lawsuit against at least one entity that provides counseling for homosexuals. The SPLC sued the non-profit group Jews Offering New Alternatives for Healing (JONAH), arguing that the conversion therapy services were a "dangerous and discredited practice that claims to convert people from gay to straight." The case was filed in November 2012 and describes how the plaintiffs – four young men and two of their parents – "were lured into JONAH's services through deceptive business practices."[122]

Using the SPLC's line of reasoning, if everyone who attends an Alcoholics Anonymous (AA) meeting is not cured of alcoholism for life, then AA is guilty of consumer fraud. In actuality, AA can establish a system based on what has worked for others, but it is up to the individual to implement the system within his or her personal life. The same is true for overcoming homosexuality.

If the SPLC wins its case, expect to see more lawsuits filed against religious groups that offer counseling to homosexuals in the future.

Rosaria Champagne Butterfield

Rosaria Champagne Butterfield, author of *The Secret Thoughts of an Unlikely Convert: An English Professor's Journey Into Christian Faith,* was a tenured English professor at Syracuse University, a skeptic about Christianity, and in a committed lesbian relationship. Her academic specialty was Queer Theory, a postmodern form of gay and lesbian studies. Today Butterfield is a mother of four, a homemaker, and wife of a Presbyterian pastor named Kent. In her book, Butterfield shares the story of her conversion from a radical lesbian to a redeemed Christian.

"I tried to toss the Bible and all of its teachings in the trash — I really tried," said Butterfield, in a Feb. 18, 2013 interview on the "Authors On the Line" podcast. "But I kept reading it, reading it not just for pleasure, but reading it because I was engaged in a research program trying to refute the religious right from a lesbian feminist perspective. . . . After my second or third, maybe fourth, pass through the entire Bible something started to happen."[123]

Kendal Richardson

Kendal Richardson (not related to the author), who wrote *Unconditional Love*, a book of poetry about his deliverance from homosexuality, discussed his experiences and transformation in an interview. After being molested at ages 4 and 8 by a neighbor who introduced him to "Playboy magazine, oral sex, shame and guilt," Richardson began engaging in homosexuality at age 16 and his life then began a downward spiral of random gay sexual encounters.

"Mall bathrooms, bus station and truck stop bathrooms, alleys, porn shops, chat lines – these are all hotbeds of gay activity," said Richardson. He went on to describe gay clubs with black rooms in the rear of the facilities where people would do "whatever they wanted in the dark." Flyers were distributed in local gay communities inviting those were interested to attend sex parties and "raw dog" parties where no condoms were used during male anal sex orgies.

Richardson became infected with HIV at age 19 through oral sex. "God found me at the age of 23," he said. "I was a prostitute at the time and God sent two men – ministers who were still in the lifestyle – to tell me to accept God into my heart." Richardson turned his life around and became an ordained minister in January 2008, starting a homosexuality deliverance ministry later that year. He speaks around the country on the topic of overcoming same-sex attractions.

"Behaviors can be changed," he said. "Any molested individual can be changed. They have to come to a realization of who they are and who God is. That's the purpose of ministry." But he emphasizes that the process does not occur overnight. "Nobody waves a magic wand. I still have a long way to go."

Natalie N. Johnson

New Orleans native Natalie N. Johnson's journey toward freedom from homosexuality started at a similar place as many others. Johnson was molested at the age of 5 or 6 by a group of boys at school during recess, and then reoccurred a year or so later. "I was so humiliated and degraded I didn't tell anyone," she says.

However, her homosexual ideations didn't begin until, while still in elementary school, she and her siblings were watching TV, channel surfing, and stumbled upon a pornography channel, which they watched when their parents were not at home. "After that, there were lustful fantasies throughout my mind that led to frequent masturbation and thoughts that were strongly homosexual," said Johnson.

As a teenager, Johnson realized she was sinning in the eyes of God, asked for forgiveness and was baptized. "But I still wasn't saved."

Johnson says she never actually had a gay sex partner and kept the homosexual thoughts to herself. "I had lust in my heart and mind. It was a sin I committed upon myself." The temptations continued to rise up occasionally and her mind "became muddled with blasphemy and thoughts of hatred toward the Lord."

She shared her concerns with her father, but without specificity, choosing instead to tell him that she no longer felt God's presence in her life. "My Dad prayed for me and told me to trust in the Lord, and the temptations went away."

Johnson still struggled with occasional urges and, when she began working for a high-end retail chain, the urges became stronger. As a result, she confessed her problems to a co-worker, who responded by praying for her in the company break room. "The Lord gave me the Holy Ghost right there on the spot and all of the depression and temptation faded away." That was five years ago, but Johnson's troubles did not end there.

She was finally able to tell her parents and other members of her family about everything that had happened to her as a little girl. Mostly, they were supportive. Johnson was overjoyed about her deliverance and began witnessing and preaching against homosexuality. This created a backlash, even among some family members. When she shared her testimony and posted her confession on a website she frequented, Deviantart.com, the backlash was swift and fierce.

Although she has adjusted to the reality that not everyone will be receptive to her exhortations, she disagrees with those who claim that change is impossible. "The idea that you are born that way and cannot be delivered – that's all lies."

The Influence of Amazon.com

Amazon.com entered the political arena with both feet on the issue of gay marriage in July 2012 when its founder, Jeff Bezos, contributed $2.5 million to defend Washington's gay marriage law.[124] The company's advocacy of gay marriage continued with its Kindle Paperwhite television advertisement which premiered in February 2013.

The Amazon ad opens with a young man and woman on the beach discussing how sunlight affected the screens on their e-readers. The female uses the Amazon Paperwhite, which she describes as "perfect at the beach," adding that "with the built-in light, I can read anywhere, anytime." The inference from the very beginning of the commercial is that their meeting is a potential love connection.

The gentleman then purchases the Amazon Paperwhite online using his tablet and suggests that they celebrate. "My husband's bringing me a drink right now," she says, and the man replies, "so is mine," referring to his "husband." Then the camera pans to two men standing at the bar and waving: one is her husband and the other is *his* husband.

By the end of the commercial, the viewer understands Amazon's message with crystal clarity: Having a husband is no longer the exclusive privilege of a female; a male can have a husband, too, if gay marriage is legalized. The fact that Bezos has also contributed millions of dollars to the campaign to legalize gay marriage makes his industry prominence all the more relevant.

Due to Amazon.com's dominance as an online purveyor of books and literature, its book review system can be as powerful as any national media outlet in terms of influence on a book's validity and sales. And with the announcement that Amazon.com founder, Jeff Bezos, purchased the burgeoning *Washington Post* newspaper in August 2013, that influence will likely grow.

An examination of Amazon.com reviews for books on the topic of deliverance from homosexuality reveals an interesting pattern: Any book that challenges or opposes the prevailing "gay for life" position among gay activists receives a 1-star review on Amazon.com, especially those books that are written by authors who have overcome homosexual ideations and behavior. Many gay activists apply these 1-star ratings to books that they apparently haven't even read. David Wilkins, who reviewed the book *Leaving Homosexuality: A Practical Guide for Men and Women Looking for a Way Out* by Alan Chambers, admitted in his review that he didn't read the book (other than the first few pages, which are available free online), but gave it a 1-star rating anyway.[125]

It is virtually impossible to review a book one hasn't read. But that didn't stop Wilkins and others from applying low ratings to this book and others like it. In fact, after an examination of several books listed on Amazon on this topic and the reviews of those who rated them with 1 star, 99.9 percent of the reviewers were not verified purchasers of any of the books, making the odds that any of these naysayers actually read and purchased the books remote.

One reviewer, Brittany T. Correa, had posted reviews on several books about deliverance from homosexuality and essentially wrote a similarly-worded review about them all. "There is no such thing as coming out of homosexuality," Correa wrote about the book, *Coming Out of Homosexuality: New Hope for Men and Women* by Bob Davies and Lori Rentzel. "This kind of book teaches people to deny who they are."[126]

But her statement is simply untrue for those people whose homosexual thoughts commenced as a result of molestation, experimentation or watching pornography. Since those people went into homosexuality through an entryway of a traumatic experience, the reverse would also have to be true: They can, indeed, exit from the same door, and many have done so.

"People can launch and do launch orchestrated campaigns" of online reviews of books, products and businesses," says Frank Bruni, op-ed columnist for *The New York Times*.[127] These reviews can have a tremendous impact on perceptions of a book's credibility and, ultimately, on sales. The knowledge of this impact leads some gay activists to launch campaigns against those whose opinion differs from theirs.

Thousands of Individuals Have Been Delivered Through Spiritual Transformation

For those interested in viewing testimonies of individuals who have been delivered from homosexuality utilizing Christian techniques of prayer, meditation, change of environment and self-discipline, the following YouTube channel includes dozens of videos on this topic. The testimonies are extremely detailed and transparent.

http://www.youtube.com/watch?v=XF1ZbOMjg34&list=PL0DAFD0C403690D56

The confessions shine a spotlight on the aspect of homosexuality that the media does not expose and that is the random sexual encounters, especially among male homosexuals, that occur in men's restrooms and other public places, often multiple times per day. Viewing pornography at an early age, especially gay pornography, is also a common thread.

Sadly, the vast majority of the confessions reference childhood molestation and/or rape, in many cases by a family member. College years are frequently the years of increased sexual activity, discovery and experimentation.

Depression, self-loathing and suicidal ideations are common. Most of the individuals didn't have a father in the home, pointing to the influence that the breakdown of the family has had on the increase in homosexual activity. The concept that making a change was not easy was universal among them, but they also say that homosexuality is, indeed, a *choice*.

Gay activists, aided by the media, insist upon denying the existence or sincerity of these individuals. But the truth that they do not want the public to know is that, if one person can be changed, it means that others can also be delivered from homosexuality *if they have the desire* and they select a method that actually works.

If gay activists really care about the well-being of gay individuals, they would realize they are doing a disservice and causing irreparable harm to people who were molested as children, began to question their sexuality, but ultimately want to be the heterosexuals God created them to be. But these activists may succeed in getting politicians to ban all counseling programs which offer these services, even the ones that are offered by churches and religious institutions. If religious leaders work with gay activists to craft legislation legalizing gay marriage, and wish to include a religious exemption, they should ensure that ministers, churches and others which offer this type of counseling are protected.

CHAPTER 8
EVERYTHING'S COMING UP ROSES

Although media are known far and wide for their focus on negativity, for some reason, they hardly ever seem to report negative stories about gay individuals, organizations, or lobbying groups. Nearly all of the coverage about gay individuals and groups is positive, making the public believe that they are all in long-term relationships, are model citizens, raise perfect children, commit no crimes and that the actions in which they engage never have negative consequences.

Here is the narrative that the national media consistently promote regarding homosexuality and gay marriage:

- All homosexuals are in loving, monogamous, long-term relationships and simply want to marry who they love.
- Children in households headed by gays/lesbians are well adjusted and have no ill effects from their home environment.
- Homosexuals do not engage in any negative, promiscuous behaviors, nor are there any health consequences associated with gay male sexual intimacy.

Reports that contradict the above storyline rarely see the light of day. The facts, however, are quite different. The majority of homosexuals do not appear to be interested in tying the proverbial knot and prefer to remain single. Some homosexuals are promiscuous, the same as is true for heterosexuals. Some homosexuals have sexually transmitted diseases, just like heterosexuals. Some homosexuals commit crimes, just like heterosexuals. Despite the picture of perfection about gay individuals and gay culture the media like to paint, homosexuals are human, like the rest of us, with all of the human frailties, shortcomings, successes and failures we all experience. There are good and bad elements in every group, but viewers never see a balanced picture of life within gay culture.

Regarding the percentage of homosexuals who are interested in getting married, according to recent data released by the U.S. Census Bureau, in the last 15 years, only 150,000 same-sex couples have elected to take advantage of marriage privileges in states where these unions have been legalized — equivalent to around one in five of the self-identified same-sex couples in the United States.[128]

In New York City, for example, when gay marriage became legal in 2011, officials devised a lottery system to handle the much-anticipated onslaught of thousands of marriage applications for genderless marriage. They projected they could handle a total of 2,500 marriages on July 24, 2011, the first day gay marriage was legal. But by the time the 48-hour lottery had closed, only 823 couples had signed up – less than one-third of the anticipated demand – and many of those couples were from other states.[129]

In the first year when gay marriage was an option in Massachusetts, the first state that legalized gay marriage, more than 6,100 same-sex couples were married and that number included many couples from other states. Pent-up demand in the first year resulted in a number of marriages for gay couples that was much greater than it would be in subsequent years. The numbers fell dramatically to only 2,060 the second year, and was about 1,500 in 2006 and 2007.[130]

In 2008, Massachusetts experienced an uptick in gay marriages and in 2009, the number had grown to 2,814. Since then, however, the number of gay marriages has declined each year, which could be a reflection of legalized gay marriage in other states in the Northeast, eliminating the necessity for gay couples in the region who wish to marry having to travel to Massachusetts to do so.[131]

Interestingly, among gay couples in Massachusetts, female/female marriages exceeded those of gay males by at least 55 percent every year. From these lopsided numbers, one could conclude that lesbians are more interested in establishing permanent, long-term relationships than are their gay male counterparts.[132]

The same pattern of an initial rush for large numbers of gay couples to marry during the first year gay marriage became legal, with a subsequent dramatic drop-off in subsequent years, also occurred in other countries that legalized gay marriage. In the Netherlands, where gay marriage has been legal since 2001, the practice is actually declining in popularity: 2,500 gay couples married in 2001, 1,800 in 2002, and the numbers have been dwindling ever since.[133]

Moreover, in countries where gay marriage has been legal for at least a decade, gay unions have considerably higher divorce rates than do those of heterosexuals. In Norway, male same-sex marriages are 50 percent more likely to end in divorce than heterosexual marriages, and female same-sex marriages are a whopping 167 percent more likely to be dissolved. Similar results have been noted in Sweden, where the divorce risk for male-male partnerships is 50 percent higher than for heterosexual marriages, and the divorce risk for female partnerships is nearly double that for men.[134]

Suffer the Little Children...

Since it is biologically impossible for two homosexuals to conceive a child and procreate together, same-sex households with children can only be formed in one of four ways:

1. One of the partners had children through a prior relationship with someone of the opposite gender;
2. Adoption;
3. Sperm donation; or
4. Surrogate mother.

In recent years, the national media and gay activists have painted an idyllic image regarding children raised in households with gay parents. To bolster their argument, they have emphasized a few studies whose results claim that children raised in households with gay parents experience no ill-effects from their environment. In fact, these studies suggest that children raised with gay parents may be *better off* than those raised by heterosexuals.

Ezra Klein of *The Washington Post* seemed to agree in his March 29, 2013 blog: "The clear and consistent consensus in the social science profession is that across a wide range of indicators, children fare just as well when they are raised by same-sex parents when compared to children raised by opposite-sex parents."[135]

This statement strains credulity. When one peels away the layers of half-truths and junk science and examines the methodology of these so-called studies, a different conclusion will likely be reached. Concern has been raised in the scientific community about the quality of these studies. In particular, most are based on non-random, non-representative data often employing small samples that do not allow for generalization to the large population of gay and lesbian families.[136]

According to sociologist Mark Regnerus of the University of Texas at Austin, most gay parenting research compares gay and lesbian parenting to single, divorced, and step-parent parenting, or conversely compares a select, and often socio-economically privileged, population of gay parents to a broad, representative sample of the general population. In addition, these studies have focused on the responses of parents for their views about what it is like to be parenting as a gay man or lesbian woman, rather than the views of the adult children raised in these households.[137]

One notable example of the failure to use random sampling in these studies is the National Longitudinal Lesbian Family Study (NLLFS), analyses of which were prominently featured in the media in 2011. The NLLFS employs a convenience sample, recruited entirely by self-selection from announcements posted "at lesbian events, in women's bookstores, and in lesbian newspapers" in Boston, Washington and San Francisco. Samples collected using this methodology reveal an inherent bias.[138]

In addition, the studies compare children raised in households with gay couples to those of children whose heterosexual parents are divorced. Social science has already established that children who are a product of divorce tend to have challenges with emotional maladjustments and insecurity. And those effects are usually long-term.[139]

Nearly every credible social science study conducted has shown that the most ideal circumstance to raise a child is in a household where the child's biological parents are married to each other. Rutgers University sociologist David Popenoe has called married-biological parents "the gold standard for insuring optimal outcomes in a child's development."[140]

And, as stated before, despite same-sex couples' efforts to produce children using sperm donors and surrogate mothers, only a heterosexual couple can biologically produce a child together. A child raised by a same-sex couple does not, nor will he or she ever, possess the genes of both "parents."

But one does not have to be a social scientist to conclude that children raised by two women or two men will exhibit some behavioral and socialization differences when compared to children raised by their biological mother and father. In addition, they will experience some feelings of loss and crisis of identity regarding the biological parent they may have never met, similar to the feelings experienced by an adopted child. Common sense is all that is required to draw such a conclusion.

Klein and other media representatives also choose to ignore the detailed, heartfelt biographical accounts provided by adult children of same-sex couples. Despite what gay activists and media representatives would like the public to believe, many of these children are suffering from emotional and psychological trauma. Although some are afraid to come forward because of the certain attacks they will have to endure from gay activists, not all of them have been silenced.

Dr. Robert Oscar Lopez, who teaches at California State University at Northridge, was raised by his lesbian mother and her partner. He wrote a detailed, heartfelt commentary published in 2012 that described his upbringing, early adulthood and his challenges adjusting to a world that, unlike his childhood household, is half male and half female.

> Quite simply, growing up with gay parents was very difficult, and not because of prejudice from neighbors. People in our community didn't really know what was going on in [my] house. To most outside observers, I was a well-raised, high-achieving child, finishing high school with straight A's.
>
> Inside, however, I was confused. When your home life is so drastically different from everyone around you, in a fundamental way striking at basic physical relations, you grow up weird. I have no mental health disorders or

biological conditions. I just grew up in a house so unusual that I was destined to exist as a social outcast.

My peers learned all the unwritten rules of decorum and body language in their homes; they understood what was appropriate to say in certain settings and what wasn't; they learned both traditionally masculine and traditionally feminine social mechanisms.[141]

The answer most gay activists offer for Lopez' childhood dilemma is to eliminate traditional gender roles and mores entirely or, at a minimum, blur the lines to the point where the characteristics and roles are largely indistinguishable. In other words, in their view, society is at fault for being so rigid and anachronistic.

Lopez describes a life of childhood confusion, since he had no male role model and "[his] mother and her partner were both unlike traditional fathers or traditional mothers. . .My home life was not traditional nor conventional. I suffered because of it, in ways that are difficult for sociologists to index."[142]

Even the simplest tasks, such as how to dress or present himself in an attractive way to girls, became an issue for Lopez. In college, he was presumed to be gay by observers and came out as bisexual. But he was portrayed by the LGBT group on his college campus, who insisted he was definitely a homosexual, as a liar who "just wasn't ready to come out of the closet as gay yet."[143]

He avoids claiming to be "straight" because of the backlash from gay activists that is almost certain to occur, even though he started out uncertain about his sexuality and eventually found himself in a relationship with a woman. "I don't feel like dealing with gay activists skewering me the way they go on search-and-destroy missions against ex-gays, "closet cases," or "homocons," Lopez writes.

To support his contention that children raised by gay parents do, indeed, experience significant behavioral challenges, Lopez cites the Regnerus study.[144]

"Growing up different from other people is difficult," writes Lopez, "and the difficulties raise the risk that children will develop maladjustments or self-medicate with alcohol and other dangerous behaviors. Each of those 248 [in the study of adult children of parents who had same-sex romantic relationships] is a human story, no doubt with many complexities."[145]

The Regnerus study further validates Lopez's experiences. The study found that the children who were raised by a gay or lesbian parent as little as 15 years ago were usually conceived within a heterosexual marriage, which then dissolved due to divorce or separation, leaving the child with a single parent. That parent then had at least one same-sex romantic relationship, sometimes outside of the child's home, sometimes within it.[146]

Among those respondents who grew up with a lesbian mother or a gay father, less than 1 percent spent a span of 18 years with the same "two mothers" or "two fathers." These study results strongly suggest that the parents' same-sex relationships were often short-lived, a finding consistent with the broader research on elevated levels of instability among same-sex romantic partners.[147]

Although Lopez describes himself as bisexual, he is against redefining marriage to include individuals of the same gender. Children raised by same-sex parents "deeply feel the loss of a father or mother, no matter how much we love our gay parents," writes Lopez.[148]

These children also "feel disconnected from the gender cues of people around them," Lopez continues, and they long for a role model of the opposite sex.

Regarding the sexual orientation of children raised in households where the parents are the same gender, Lopez believes this environment most certainly has an impact, despite the proclamations of gay activists to the contrary. "I would posit that children raised by same-sex couples are naturally going to be more curious about and experimental with homosexuality without necessarily being pure of any attraction to the opposite sex."[149]

As is the case with any individual who does not agree with the dual mantras that all gays are born that way and none can ever change, leaders within the LGBT community largely dismiss Lopez's experiences and assertions.

Sperm-Donor Kids

Lesbian couples will often establish families by having one of the two women involved undergo artificial insemination by a sperm donor. The children born from these relationships will have two mothers (although, technically there is still one mother and one father, the sperm donor) and will be raised in households where no adult male resides.

Each year an estimated 30,000 to 60,000 children are born via artificial insemination, but exact numbers are hard to come by. Neither the fertility industry nor any other entity is required to report on these statistics. The practice is not regulated and the children's health and well-being are not tracked.[150]

Acquiring a sperm donor is essentially a financial transaction and the parent or parents involved are not required to undergo background checks and evaluations as is the case for adoptive parents. Any woman with the financial resources to purchase sperm from a sperm bank can become a mother, regardless of the sort of home life she may provide for the child.

In adoption, prospective parents go through a thorough, systematic review, including home visits and detailed questions about their relationship, finances and even their sex life. If there are any red flags, the couple might not get the child. With donor conception, the state requires absolutely none of that.[151]

Researchers Karen Clark and Elizabeth Marquardt joined forces with professor Norval Glenn of the University of Texas at Austin and conducted a study focusing on young-adult donor offspring. The study of 18- to 45-year-olds includes 485 who were conceived via sperm donation, 562 adopted as infants and 563 raised by their biological parents.[152]

The results reveal that family structures resulting from sperm donation – which represent the method used by a substantial percentage of lesbian couples to achieve procreation -- are not the model of perfection gay activists would have the public believe. Nearly half of adult donor offspring are disturbed that money was involved in the actions that led to their conception. More than half say that when they see someone who resembles them, they wonder if they are related. About two-thirds affirm the right of donor offspring to know the truth about their origins.[153]

Moreover, regardless of socioeconomic status, donor offspring are twice as likely as those raised by biological parents to report problems with the law before age 25. They are more than twice as likely to report having struggled with substance abuse. And they are about 1.5 times as likely to report depression or other mental health problems.[154]

Researchers Clark and Marquardt concluded: "Listening to the stories of donor-conceived adults, you begin to realize there's really no such thing as a 'donor.' Every child has a biological father. To claim otherwise is simply to compound the pain. . ."

In other words, gay couplings and other arrangements which require sperm donation deprive the child who is ultimately conceived the natural human instinct we all have to know the identities of our parents. As a remedy, Clark and Marquardt suggest that the U.S. follow the lead of Britain, Norway, Sweden and other nations and end the anonymous trade of sperm. That measure could solve the part of the problem regarding parental identity, but not the emotional uneasiness about how the donor offspring were conceived in the first place.

Surrogate Mothers, a/k/a "Ovens"

In the same way that sperm donation is a financial transaction designed to result in procreation, so is the act of hiring a surrogate mother to carry a baby to term for a couple –

homosexual or heterosexual -- that cannot conceive. Gay male couples who want to have children will often use the sperm of one of the males and select a surrogate mother for in vitro fertilization. *Washington Post* columnist Kathleen Parker writes: "There is a dark underbelly to the surrogacy industry – and it is a business – including a burgeoning industry that preys on vulnerable women, commodifying them as 'ovens.'"[155]

As for the children, it is possible for them to have as many as five "parents," from the egg and sperm donors, to the woman who carries them to the couple or single parent who adopts them, says Parker.[156] Children born under such circumstances are likely to have identity crises as adults, when they begin to search for the genetic origins of their existence.

In many of these scenarios, the woman is nothing more than a "breeder," in Parker's view, reminiscent of the era of American slavery when black women were purchased by slave masters for their ability to bear children. The mother must be willing to stay in the same geographic location until the baby is born and, of course, surrender rights to the child. In other words, the baby becomes a mere commodity and the surrogate mother is simply the conduit.

Although surrogate mothers are compensated financially for their role in the process, there is an emotional price exacted for agreeing to carry someone else's child. As a mother, I cannot imagine carrying a baby to term and then handing it over to someone else. There is a strong, natural emotional connection between mother and baby that occurs nearly from the time of conception. By the time the mother can feel the baby moving in the womb, the anticipation of the child's birth becomes stronger and the emotional ties increase.

In order for a surrogate mother to be willing to relinquish her parental rights, she would need to disconnect these emotions early in the pregnancy. Actions that mothers would normally do for a child they intend to keep, such as talking to or singing to the baby while still in the womb – both of which have proven to be beneficial to a child's well-being and intelligence after birth – are almost certainly abandoned.

"Human babies are not things; their mothers are not ovens," concludes Parker. "But bartering and selling babies-to-order sure make them seem that way. By turning the miracle of life into a profit-driven, state-regulated industry, the stork begins to resemble a vulture."[157]

Health Risks for Gays and Lesbians

Despite gay activists' pronouncements to the contrary, there are several health risks associated with gay male intimacy. For most heterosexuals, the idea of gay male sex is something they would prefer not to discuss or visualize, so it is convenient for media to exclude reports about these health risks from their list of issues about which they report. However, these risks are real and can shorten the life spans of those who engage in gay male intimacy.

First, although media do not cover stories HIV and AIDS with the same frequency they once did, it is still a fact that gay or bisexual men who have sex with men (MSM) are the most severely affected population. According to the National Institute of Drug Abuse, MSM account for just a small fraction (2 percent) of the total U.S. population, yet nearly two-thirds of all new infections occurred within this group in 2009, and one-half of all people living with HIV in 2008 were MSM.[158]

A number of sexually transmitted diseases can be transferred as a result of what medical professionals refer to as "receptive anal intercourse." Polymicrobial infection is common and there is an overlap in symptoms caused by the organisms that may infect the anorectum. Gonorrhea, campylobacter, chlamydia, shigella, chancroid, granuloma inguinale and syphilis are all diseases that are transmitted via anal intercourse. Manifestations of these and other diseases that result from anal intercourse include anal ulcerations, proctitis, erythema, edema, bacteremia, arthritis, dermatitis, bloody diarrhea, myalgias, chills, fever, abdominal pain and cramping.[159]

There are additional health risks involved with gay and lesbian relationships. The American Journal of Public Health has published reports based on studies conducted among gay males and lesbian females and reached the following conclusions:

- Hispanic lesbians and bisexual women, compared with Hispanic heterosexual women, were at elevated risk for disparities in smoking, asthma, and disability. Hispanic bisexual women also showed higher odds of arthritis, acute drinking, poor general health and frequent mental distress compared with Hispanic heterosexual women.[160]
- Gay and lesbian youth were on average two times more likely to experience sexual abuse, parental physical abuse or assault at school or to miss school through fear.[161]

- The prevalence of disability is higher among lesbian, gay and bisexual adults compared with their heterosexual counterparts; lesbian, gay and bisexual adults with disabilities are significantly younger than heterosexual adults with disabilities.[162]
- Gay and lesbian youth were at about double a greater risk of post-traumatic stress disorder (PTSD) than heterosexuals. Child abuse victimization disparities accounted for one third to one half of PTSD disparities by sexual orientation.[163]
- African-American men who have sex with men and women (bisexuals) and reported higher levels of gender role conflict (GRC) than other study participants also reported more psychological distress, lower self-esteem, greater internalized homophobia, less HIV knowledge, lower risk reduction skills, less disclosure of same-sex behaviors to others, and more unprotected vaginal and anal intercourse with female partners.[164]

Moreover, the Regnerus study mentioned previously, found that, when asked if they were ever touched sexually by a parent or other adult, the children of lesbian mothers were 11 times more likely to say "yes" than the children from an intact biological family, and the children of gay fathers were three times more likely to say "yes." This same study asked respondents to identify their sexual orientation and found that children of lesbian mothers were more open to same-sex romantic relationships, bisexuality, and asexuality than any other group. Children of gay fathers were the next least likely to identify as fully heterosexual. Children from intact biological families were most likely of all family types to identify as entirely heterosexual. In other words, the type of household in which a child is raised *does* have an impact on whether or not they gravitate toward homosexuality.[165]

The above-mentioned results from government health agencies and other research entities demonstrate that there are factors and risks that may have a medical, psychological and/or sociological impact on those who are involved in same-sex relationships, and on children who are raised in same-sex parented households. In the same way that individuals in the general population are not immune from the consequences of their actions, gay individuals also cannot avoid the ramifications associated with being practicing homosexuals.

Atlantic Magazine Takes a Giant Leap Into Fantasy

Most national media outlets portray individuals living in the gay community as having an almost utopian existence with long-term, loving relationships, near-perfect children and little to no health challenges. But one media entity, *Atlantic Magazine*, takes the portrayal a step further by asserting that same-sex couples can teach heterosexuals a thing or two about what it means to be in a committed relationship.

With the front cover of its June 2013 edition titled, "What Straights Can Learn From Same-Sex Couples," and the article heading of "The Gay Guide to Wedded Bliss," *Atlantic* takes a giant leap into the world of fantasy with the premise that, after having experienced only ten years of legalized marriage in a few American states (versus thousands of years for traditional marriage), gay couples have discovered all of the answers to what makes a marriage work.[166]

The first noticeable aspect of the article is its length. The writer, Liza Mundy, uses more than 10,000 words to present her argument. Moreover, the editor uses a subheading for the article that matches the boldness of the edition's cover: "Research Finds That Same-Sex Unions Are Happier Than Heterosexual Marriages. What Can Gay and Lesbian Couples Teach Straight Ones About Living in Harmony?" One could easily have a laugh-out-loud moment when reading such a ridiculous assertion but, because of my curiosity as to what the writer could possibly use for evidence, I decided to forge ahead and read the treatise.

After liberals and progressives have spent the better part of the last 50 years undermining traditional marriage by equating the woman's role in these relationships as tantamount to bondage, the article's writer seemed surprised that the institution has become endangered. "It is more than a little ironic that gay marriage has emerged as the era's defining civil-rights struggle even as marriage itself seems more endangered every day," Mundy wrote, as she went on to describe the sad state of traditional marriage in the new millennium. Her solution? We should all listen to the "wisdom" of same-sex couples, who have experienced marriage for what amounts to about five minutes when compared to the complete annals of human history.

Reading the article takes a bit of navigation because Mundy insists upon jettisoning the concepts of marriage and parenting as we've known them to be since the beginning of mankind, and redefining these institutions using as many descriptive terms as possible. Since, in the new world order we can no longer assume that a child's mom and dad are female and male, Mundy unveils the newfangled terminology: "Opposite-sex couples," "straight mothers," "same-sex dads," "lesbian mothers," "gay dads," "gay-male couples," "straight couples," and "straight groom," are now among the contemporary ways to describe parents.[167]

Using descriptive language, Mundy reinforces her assertion that same-sex couples have an avant-garde approach while those in traditional marriages are antiquated. In her view, those in male/female marriages are "rigid," "anachronistic," "old-fashioned," and "afflicted," and their relationships are "negative," "inequitable," "lopsided," and "burdensome." Conversely, she describes gay relationships as "enlightened," "egalitarian," "more cooperative," and "mutually hands-on," and the partners within these relationships as "less belligerent and less domineering."[168]

As for the impact of gay marriage on traditional marriage, Mundy makes a number of arguments, none of which can be supported by facts. On the one hand, she contends there will be no impact at all, referring to a statement made by Gary Gates, demographer at the Williams Institute, a gay advocacy research center affiliated with the UCLA School of Law. "The notion that this group [same-sex couples] can somehow fundamentally change the institution of marriage – I find it difficult to wrap my head around," said Gates. Of course, that question has yet to be answered since gay marriage in the U.S. is a novel experiment with no parallel to which outcomes can be compared.[169]

Mundy also argues that perhaps the boom of publicity around same-sex weddings "could awaken among heterosexuals a new interest in the institution, at least for a time." This argument defies logic. If a man is considering proposing to his girlfriend, it is highly unlikely that the specter of two men on the way to the altar would motivate him to pop the question. But Mundy seems to be undeterred by the absence of logic. As evidence for her argument, Mundy cites interviews with two Unitarian ministers with small congregations in the Washington, D.C. area, and a vendor at a wedding expo, who all suggested they had seen an increase in wedding activity in the year since gay marriage was legalized in the District of Columbia.[170]

But, if Mundy really wants some reliable data, she could examine the marriage rates among male/female couples in Massachusetts since gay marriage was legalized in 2004. Those statistics completely rebut Mundy's argument since the number of male/female marriages has actually decreased in the state every year since gay marriage was legalized. The only exception is the year 2010, which showed a slight increase from the year before, but the numbers continued to go down in the subsequent years 2011 and 2012.[171]

It is doubtful that the decrease in traditional marriages in Massachusetts was a direct result of the implementation of gay marriage. Other factors were likely involved, such as the shifts in demographics in the state as related to age (the median age of Massachusetts residents is 36.5), and the state's flat population growth. But opponents of gay marriage do not argue that the impact on traditional marriage will be direct and immediate, but rather indirect and long-term, so the statistics are irrelevant either way.

To support her premise that the relationships between same-sex partners are superior, Mundy cites a number of studies, all of which are biased or limited in scope. She refers to "a growing body of scholarship on household division of labor" which shows that "in many ways, same-sex couples do it better." One study by sociologist Pepper Schwartz and her gay colleague, the late Philip Blumstein, concluded that "gay and lesbian couples were fairer in their dealings with one another than straight couples, both in intent and in practice." How these two intellectuals could draw such a sweeping conclusion is puzzling, to say the least.

Mundy also cites a study by psychologist Esther Rothblum of San Diego State University, herself a lesbian, in which civil-union couples were asked to identify one of their heterosexual siblings who was married, and they all participated in the research. This study follows the pattern of bias in most surveys of same-sex couples:

1) No random sampling is used and participants are self-selected, and

2) The research is conducted by someone who is gay; therefore, the researcher has a stake in the outcome.

The *Atlantic* article was also contradictory in at least one contention. According to Mundy, lesbians tend to discuss things endlessly, "achieving a degree of closeness unmatched by the other types of couples." But she later writes: "Lesbian couples seem to be more likely to break up than gay ones." In other words, according to Mundy, lesbian couples are simultaneously most likely to be happy with their relationships and also most disgruntled.[172]

Mundy was able to identify one woman in a traditional marriage who seemed to be disappointed that her husband didn't act more like a lesbian female in terms of his views on the roles of husband and wife in the home. But it is unlikely that her husband would ever possess the same attitudes and motivations as a lesbian because, despite what Mundy and other gay activists would have all of us believe, men and women *are* different.

Monogamy: That's So Yesterday

Surprisingly, the issue of monogamy, or the lack thereof, among gay males is discussed in detail in Mundy's article. According to researcher Schwartz, "Among gay men, a whopping 82 percent. . .reported having had sex outside their relationship." Under normal circumstances, this level of infidelity would be labeled "promiscuous," but since gay activists consider it anathema to suggest that their lifestyle has elements of promiscuity, Mundy uses a different approach.

She argues that monogamy isn't really all that important to the success of a relationship and seems to support the argument of gay rights activist Dan Savage that monogamy can do a couple more harm than good. Savage and others have coined a new term for allowing each partner in the relationship to have occasional dalliances – "monagamish." No mention was made of the impact of eschewing the ideal of a committed relationship and the issue of sexually transmitted diseases. The standard for marriage is simply lowered and whatever consequences may result are merely ignored.[173]

Gay activists frequently pose the question: If a loving couple who just happens to be gay wants to get married, how does it hurt your [or traditional] marriage? Here is a prime example of how the redefinition of marriage to include any two persons weakens the overall institution. It starts with the language used and the need to continually redefine marriage away from its roots as a long-term, until-death-do-us-part relationship into one where each of the individuals is easily replaced or where additional partners are added.

Besides the term "monagamish," the terms "polyamory," "throuple," and "wedlease" have recently been introduced into popular culture. In August 2013, the progressive online journal *Salon* posted the account of Angi Becker Stevens and her shared life with a husband, boyfriend, and daughter under the headline "My two husbands." The article's subhead: "Everyone wants to know how my polyamorous family works. You'd be surprised how normal we really are."[174]

The Showtime cable network created a show called "Polyamory: Married and Dating," which, in 2013, was in its second season. The show follows two polyamorous families living in Southern California. In season two, Chris, his wife Leigh Ann and their girlfriend Megan are a threesome living in Hollywood. According to the Showtime website, when Leigh Ann and Chris both fell in love with Megan, they suddenly found themselves in a polyamorous relationship.[175]

The word "throuple," which is similar to "couple," is now being used to describe a relationship among three people. The word appeared in a June 29, 2012 article in *New York Magazine* that described a specific "throuple" this way:

> Their throuplehood is more or less a permanent domestic arrangement. The three men work together, raise dogs together, sleep together, miss one another, collect art together, travel together, bring each other glasses of water, and, in general, exemplify a modern, adult relationship.[176]

> When the relationship started, the three would have sex several times a week. The arrangement offered a titillating enhancement of sexual permutations. These days, as with most long-term relationships, the lovemaking has slowed. . .The throuple rarely has sex as a threesome anymore.[177]

Florida estate planning lawyer Paul Rampell introduced the term "wedlease" into the zeitgeist in an op-ed published in the Aug. 4, 2013 edition of *The Washington Post*. Rampell argues that marriage is a legal partnership that lasts a lifetime – a term that, in his view, is much too long. His remedy: Instead of wedlock, create a "wedlease." Here's how the lease could potentially work:

> Two people commit themselves to marriage for a period of years – one year, five years, 10 years,

whatever term suits them. The marital lease could be renewed at the end of the term however many times a couple likes. It could end up lasting a lifetime if the relationship is good and worth continuing. But if the relationship is bad, the couple could go their separate ways at the end of the term.[178]

In other words, the solutions Stevens, Rampell, Mundy, and others offer to "cure" already fragile marriages is further weaken them with destabilizing quick-fixes that simply will not work. Rather, they will lead to higher divorce rates and more children who are products of shattered homes.

Mundy concludes her *Atlantic Magazine* article by making a false declaration. "The fact is, there is no such thing as traditional marriage." She describes all sorts of historical marital formulas, including those that are polygamous, contractual and illegal, specifically as it relates to African Americans who, during slavery, were not allowed to experience a Christian wedding and instead performed their own makeshift ceremonies and symbolically "jumped the broom." But Mundy's statement is patently false because, even when the marriages she described were fraught with imbalances or inequities, the common thread is that they were of the male/female variety, which is what traditional marriage means.

Media's Misleading Image

By painting a virtuous, one-dimensional picture of homosexuality and the gay community, the national media does a disservice to the American public. As stated before, no group or individual is flawless. If Americans see a complete picture regarding the issues surrounding gay marriage and homosexuality, they might reach a different conclusion. The polls would probably change, an outcome national media seem determined to avoid at all costs.

CHAPTER 9
SEE NO EVIL, HEAR NO EVIL

Over the past two decades, many gay activists have earned quite a reputation for vindictiveness and ruthless behavior against people who disagree with them on the issue of gay marriage. They send a clear and consistent message: Either support gay marriage or you will experience our wrath, and your livelihood will be at risk.

The attacks on those in opposition to gay marriage have intensified over the past few years. Anyone who gets in gay advocates' way is subject to public ridicule, demotion, ostracism, or worse. In the words of author Ben Shapiro, who wrote the book *Bullies: How the Left's Culture of Fear and Intimidation Silences America*, for gay bullies, "There is only the right way (wave the rainbow flag!) and the wrong way (kids need a mom and dad)."[179] Yet, media turn a blind eye toward these acts of vandalism and violence, as well as extortion and blackmail, a tactic which I call "financial terrorism." The attitude of the media seems to be that anything goes as long as a gay activist is protesting against perceived "homophobia."

Direct confrontation with gay activists is not a prerequisite for being a target of their venomous verbal assaults. Taking a public stand in support of traditional marriage is all that is required to raise their ire.

Challenging gay activists on the issue of gay marriage is the equivalent of walking into a buzz saw or putting your foot in a huge fire ant hill. The pain is severe and some people acquiesce simply to avoid being targeted by what, in effect, is an LGBT gestapo. Yet media are deaf, dumb and blind when it relates to these actions. The list of victims is too long to enumerate them all, but here are some of the more egregious cases that have occurred in recent years.

In 2008 following the presidential election, former NFL Indianapolis Colts coach Tony Dungy withdrew his name from consideration for President Obama's advisory council on faith-based groups following pressure from gay activists. Dungy, it seems, had the audacity to endorse a ban on same-sex marriage in Indiana.

Proposition 8 Donors Targeted

That same year, Proposition 8, which was a measure to ban gay marriage in California, was on the ballot. The measure was approved by a majority of the voters. But, not willing to accept the outcome or be satisfied to battle the measure in court, gay activists obtained the records of those who contributed to the Proposition 8 effort. Two high-profile individuals were forced to resign their positions because they had made a contribution to the effort, which is their constitutional right.

Richard Raddon, the director of the Los Angeles Film Festival, contributed $1,500 to the campaign. Raddon is a member of the Mormon Church, which actively called on its congregants to work for the passage of Proposition 8. After Raddon's contribution was made public online, he offered to step down as festival director, but the board, which includes Don Cheadle, Forest Whitaker, Lionsgate President Tom Ortenberg and Fox Searchlight President Peter Rice, gave him a unanimous vote of confidence.[180]

However, gay activists were not satisfied and demanded their pound of flesh. They also berated Raddon personally via phone calls and emails. The recriminations ultimately were too much for Raddon and, when he offered to resign again, this time the board accepted. "I'm personally saddened by the outcome," said Film Independent board member Bill Condon, the writer-director of "Dreamgirls." "Someone has lost his job and possibly his livelihood because of privately held religious beliefs. I think the organization was ready to tough this out, but Rich ultimately decided it wasn't worth the cost. I'm not sure he was right."[181]

But there was another casualty in the California arts community as a result of the Proposition 8 outcome. Scott Eckern, the artistic director of the California Musical Theater, a major nonprofit production company, was also forced to resign his position after it became known that he contributed $1,000 to support the measure. Eckern is also a Mormon, and he suffered other repercussions as well.[182]

Marc Shaiman, the Tony Award-winning composer of "Hairspray," called Eckern and said he would not let his work be performed in the theater. "I was uncomfortable with money made off my work being used to put discrimination in the Constitution," said Shaiman, who is gay.

Even those who gave small donations to Proposition 8 were targeted. Margie Christoffersen, manager at El Coyote, a landmark restaurant on Los Angeles' Beverly Boulevard, donated $100 in support of Proposition 8. Christoffersen is a devout Mormon and never advertised her politics or religion in the restaurant, but her donation showed up on lists of "for" and "against" donors and the restaurant became a target.[183]

A boycott of the restaurant was organized on the Internet, unfavorable reviews of the restaurant were posted online, and throngs of angry protesters arrived at the eatery's doors. El Coyote is owned by Christoffersen's 92-year-old mother and the manager took a voluntary leave of absence for several weeks due to the emotional toll from the harassment. But she appears to have weathered the political storm as she is still serving as the restaurant's manager.[184]

The national media seem to hold the view that bullying is okay as long as it is directed toward people who oppose gay marriage. They treated these breaches of privacy as non-events. Had this sort of aggressive activity been directed toward gay activists, it would have been summarily denounced and received widespread media coverage.

Church Vandalized in Portland, Oregon

A gay activist group calling itself "Angry Queers" claimed responsibility for smashing the windows of a church in Portland, Oregon, known for teaching sexual morality. Tim Smith, pastor of the Mars Hill Church, said nine separate windows had been smashed in with rocks, including two beautiful 100-year-old stained glass windows. Church members say they hold to "traditional, Bible-based views on homosexuality."[185]

The Portland location of Mars Hill Church opened in September 2011, one of 14 nationwide satellites under nationally known pastor Mark Driscoll of Seattle. The church postponed its original opening date after learning LGBT activists planned a kiss-in at their first ceremony.[186]

Chick-Fil-A

Gay activists seem to have become especially emboldened after President Barack Obama changed his position in May 2012 and announced his support for gay marriage. A few months later, when Chick-Fil-A president Dan Cathy stated his support for traditional marriage in a radio interview, all hell seemed to break loose. Media representatives were in rare form, attacking Cathy for discrimination, rather than defending his right to free speech.

Gay activists started boycotting the restaurant chain, even though Chick-Fil-A had a record of fair treatment to its customers and employees. Gays and lesbians decided to hold a "kiss in" at Chick-Fil-A, a completely inappropriate response that actually backfired because few gay kissers showed up.

As a show of support for Cathy and Chick-Fil-A, radio talk show host and former Republican presidential candidate, Mike Huckabee, organized a social media campaign on Facebook requesting that those who supported traditional marriage eat at Chick-Fil-A on August 1, 2012. Within a few days, Huckabee's page had garnered over 600,000 likes.

Several Facebook pages were created as a counterattack, but they only garnered a fraction of the support that Huckabee received. One titled, "I Don't Appreciate Chick-Fil-A Every Day" received only 88 likes.

In support of Cathy's right to free speech and because I support traditional marriage, I decided to visit my local Chick-Fil-A on August 1 to show my support. Although I visited the restaurant at 3:30 p.m., after the usual busy lunch hour and before the dinner crowd arrived, business was brisk. There were many employees working behind the counter, and the lines were moving quickly. The atmosphere was upbeat and friendly, and the patrons were ethnically diverse. Some customers smiled at me in a knowing way, expressing silent support for the cause. There was a uniformed policeman on hand, just in case of a disturbance, but it seemed completely unnecessary. There were no protesters, picketers or expressions of displeasure.

In fact, in the case of Chick-Fil-A, the gay activists' tantrums may have backfired. In the end, it appears that Cathy gained much more than he lost. The end result has been a bonanza for Chick-Fil-A's business. Instead of hurting the company, gay activists may have unwittingly assured its longevity for years to come.

Although, according to a recent survey, 75 percent of LGBT individuals are boycotting Chick-Fil-A, the company is experiencing record growth and profits.[187] In 2012, Chick-Fil-A surpassed KFC in sales to become the largest chicken fast food restaurant in America. Further, Chick-Fil-A achieved higher system-wide sales than KFC despite having about a third fewer restaurants and being closed on Sundays, reflecting Chick-Fil-

A's unusually deep customer loyalty, observed QSR Magazine editor Sam Oches.[188]

The LGBT community may be inadvertently responsible for Chick-Fil-A's newfound fortunes as their attacks played a role in boosting customer loyalty. More information about how Chick-Fil-A's business has boomed will be discussed in Chapter 10.

Shooting at Family Research Council

The strong support for Chick-Fil-A seemed to incense at least one individual who, in August 2012, purchased 15 Chick-Fil-A sandwiches, took a handgun, 50 rounds of ammunition, and barged into the Family Research Council (FRC) headquarters in Washington, D.C. The gunman, Floyd Corkins, who is gay, shot the building manager who later wrestled Corkins to the ground. Fortunately, no one else was hurt.[189]

"They [FRC] endorse Chick-Fil-A and also Chick-Fil-A came out against gay marriage, so I was going to use that [the shooting] as a statement," Corkins told investigators. FRC is a pro-family organization that opposes abortion and gay marriage. Apparently, Corkins chose the FRC as his target after finding it listed as an anti-gay group on the website of the Southern Poverty Law Center (SPLC).[190] As mentioned in Chapter 4, lumping organizations that support traditional marriage with those that have orchestrated murders and acts of violence, like the Ku Klux Klan, is an egregious error the SPLC should correct immediately.

Corkins, 28, pleaded guilty to committing an act of terrorism while armed, interstate transportation of a firearm and ammunition, and assault with intent to kill while armed. As of this book's publication date, he had not yet been sentenced.

The Corkins incident received a minimal amount of coverage by the national media. But had the situation been reversed, had a gay rights organization's headquarters been attacked by an evangelical Christian, the coverage would have been extensive and prominent. The double standard regarding media's treatment of violence against those who support traditional marriage is blatant.

Death Threats in Connecticut

In April 2013, Daniel Sarno, 54, was sentenced to five years' probation for sending hundreds of threatening letters to Peter Wolfgang, executive director of the Family Institute of Connecticut. The Family Institute believes in and promotes traditional marriage and opposes same-sex marriage. Sarno, who is homosexual, included death threats in many of the letters and all were uniformly abusive.[191]

"No mercy for homophobes," one letter read. "I suggest you make your funeral arrangements real soon, Mr. Wolfgang. (I should know.)"

Another letter read, "I sure hope somebody blows you away. Yer [sic] dead."

Wolfgang said the case highlighted "a growing campaign of intimidation" by militant homosexuals who would like nothing more than to silence those who defend traditional marriage, according to the local newspaper, the *Journal Inquirer*.[192]

Attack on Belgian Archbishop

Archbishop Andre Leonard of Mechelen-Brussels was attacked by a lesbian group while speaking at a conference at the Free University of Brussels in Belgium. This also occurred in April 2013. During the attack, four bare-breasted protesters from the International FEMEN movement soaked the 72-year-old archbishop with water while he was sitting and praying, waving placards with the slogan, "Stop homophobia." In addition, their torsos were painted with slogans, including "In gay we trust."[193]

Preacher Attacked at Seattle Gay Pridefest 2013

A minister who picketed at the Seattle Gay Pridefest on June 29, 2013 was holding a sign reading "Repent or Else" and "Jesus Saves From Sin." He was exercising his Constitutional right to free speech, as do gay activists at events where the theme is one with which they disagree. However, the gay activists at the Seattle rally began to attack the minister verbally. Not satisfied with simply voicing their disagreement, they then began to attack the minister physically as several of them began pummeling him with their fists.

"A pack mentality appears to set in," reports Michelle Esteban of Seattle's KOMO TV in Seattle. "Police describe it as a melee." The incident was captured on video by an individual who attended the parade.[194]

But national media ignored this incident entirely. Local, Seattle-based media, Christian-based publications and YouTube are the primary sources for information regarding this heinous act. Had this been an attack on gay demonstrators by Christian onlookers is there any doubt it would have received broad-based national media coverage?

Defacing Dictionaries Nationwide

A group of anonymous gay activists in San Francisco is dissatisfied with the dictionary definition of marriage and have decided to take matters into their own hands. In the summer of 2013, they started going to libraries and book retailers and defacing dictionaries, pasting in their own updated definition of marriage over the original version using small stickers.[195]

In a Vimeo video posted on the group's website, www.hackmarriage.tumblr.com, others are encouraged to do the same. "Hack your own dictionaries," it says, offering a link through which users can download and print their own stickers. The *Oxford American Dictionary* currently defines marriage as "the formal union of a man and woman by which they become husband and wife."[196]

These actions amount to trespassing and destroying private property, yet national media treated these actions as if they were justifiable childish pranks. The libraries and bookstores which stock the books will have two choices: Expend resources to replace the dictionaries or keep them as is, which customers won't like because they won't want to pay full price for flawed items. Either way, the institutions will lose hundreds of dollars at each branch or location as a result of these activists' actions.

It is clear that national media intentionally exclude or minimize news items from their coverage if gay activists are shown in a negative light. They want the public to see only the good so that, when forming their opinion about gay marriage, their objections will be limited.

CHAPTER 10
SINS OF OMISSION

Most consumers believe that the media report all events that are important, those that have national significance or public policy implications. Yet, when events occur that involve the LGBT community, the national media will conveniently ignore major news items if they reflect negatively on gay rights causes or if they demonstrate that support for gay marriage is nowhere near universal.

Did you know that, in February 2013, nearly one million protesters marched in Paris, France in opposition to gay marriage? That 200,000 did so in Puerto Rico?

Regarding news in the United States, did you know that when the Supreme Court heard arguments on gay marriage in March 2013, among those demonstrating outside the Court there were far more in opposition than in support? Or that Chick-Fil-A, the company that found itself in the middle of the gay marriage maelstrom when its CEO stated publicly that he believed marriage is between a man and a woman, had revenues in 2012 that were up $500 million over the previous year and that the corporation opened 96 new locations? Or that when pollsters ask the question, "How would you define marriage?", more people say that marriage should be between a man and a woman than between people of either gender? Or that, in May 2013, the Illinois legislature could not muster enough votes to approve gay marriage?

The reason you probably have not heard about these and other newsworthy stories is that the national media simply will not give exposure to anything that challenges the idea that the entire country, and indeed the entire Western world, supports gay marriage. But major events have occurred during the past two years that might both surprise and inform you.

In February 2013, a crowd estimated at 800,000 marched in the streets of Paris, France to protest pending legislation that would legalize gay marriage. Aerial photographs of the massive crowd showed that its numbers rivaled those in attendance at an American presidential inauguration ceremony. The expanse of the marchers was from one side of the street to the other and extended for several city blocks in the French capital.

France is hardly known for having conservative values and is generally viewed as a liberal society in terms of sexual freedoms, which makes the size of the crowd all the more significant. The protestors included young people, Catholics and other French citizens who were particularly disturbed by the legislation's approval of child adoption by same-sex couples. Young parents pushing strollers and multiple generations of families thronged the rally, which focused on the right of children to a father and mother rather than two of either.[197]

Although the bill was ultimately passed in April, protests have continued and some government officials have refused to issue marriage licenses to same-sex couples. Jean-Michel Colo, mayor of the southern French town of Arcangues, is unapologetic. "Just because there's a law doesn't mean it's moral and right," Colo says. "It's a bad law, and it needs to be changed."[198]

France is known for its liberal social and economic policies, and such a march should have been widely covered by the media. This is especially true in the current political environment where it seems that "everyone" supports gay marriage.

Yet, for the most part, national media outlets gave the story limited coverage and, in some cases, did not cover the march at all. To its credit, *The New York Times* ran a story in its World section,[199] as did the Reuters news service.

Gay Marriage Protests in Puerto Rico

In March 2013, 200,000 protestors marched in San Juan, Puerto Rico against a proposition to legalize gay marriage. With its population of only 3.7 million people, as compared with 66 million in France, the size of this crowd was actually relatively larger than the one which gathered in Paris.

The event was organized by the group Puerto Rico for the Family, and was planned in just three weeks. "We are concerned that laws will be created to discriminate against the church," said Pastor Cesar Vazquez Muniz, a spokesman for the organizers. "We are concerned that public education will be used to change our children, presenting them with behaviors that parents don't think are correct."[200]

Muniz need only look to what has occurred in the United States as an example. The push to legalize gay marriage in the U.S. is ushering in an environment where attacks on Christians' beliefs are commonplace and where children are taught in schools that "Heather has two mommies."

Subsequent to the march, the Puerto Rico Supreme Court voted to bar homosexual adoption in the Commonwealth. Neither the march nor the Supreme Court's decision received widespread national media coverage.

Colombia Votes Against Gay Marriage

In April 2013, Colombian lawmakers voted against a proposed law to allow same-sex marriage. The bill was rejected by 51 to 17 votes. Conservative lawmaker Carlos Chavarro argued that the law would have been anathema to many in the predominantly Roman Catholic country and that marriage should be between a man and a woman, especially for the purposes of procreation.[201]

"A minority should not impose legislation because the Colombian state must legislate for the majority, and the majority want us to preserve the nuclear family," said Chavarro.

Support for Gay Marriage Costs Australian Prime Minister His Job

Australian Prime Minister Kevin Rudd's governing Labor Party lost elections in September 2013 and his support for gay marriage was the deciding factor. Tony Abbott's Liberal-National coalition handily defeated Rudd, bringing to an end six years of Labor Party rule. Abbott is described as "the most conservative leader Australia has had in many decades."[202]

According to Australian Christian Lobby Managing Director Lyle Shelton, "Rudd's bullying of a Christian pastor on Q&A in the final week of the campaign made Australians feel uncomfortable with the consequences of freedom of speech and freedom of belief should the law on marriage be changed."[203]

Illinois Legislature Couldn't Get Votes to Legalize Gay Marriage

The idea that gay marriage across the U.S. is inevitable made national headlines as Rhode Island, Delaware and Minnesota all passed measures to legalize same-sex marriage in May 2013. Media representatives were beating the drums of victory as Illinois seemed poised to be the next state to embrace the redefinition of marriage.

"The state of Illinois will be next," declared Chris Matthews on MSNBC's "Hardball" show after the Minnesota vote was passed. The Illinois Senate had already voted to approve the measure on a 34-21 vote on Valentine's Day, and the Democratic Governor Pat Quinn promised to sign the bill. President Obama called for its passage during a fundraiser in his home city and Chicago Mayor Rahm Emanuel was a major backer as well.[204]

But, apparently, voters in Illinois were not as enthusiastic. In the face of strong opposition from Catholic and conservative African-American church groups, supporters failed to muster enough votes in the Illinois House.

The national media's reaction: most simply ignored the story. Although he had been touting the upcoming Illinois vote on almost a daily basis on his program during the weeks leading up to its potential passage, on the day the measure failed, Matthews did not mention it at all. Had the measure passed, it would have been the leading story on his program as well as others on MSNBC. But only the victories of gay activists get widespread media attention, not the failures.

The Illinois legislature may revisit the issue of gay marriage in the fall of 2013. However, according to news reports, few, if any, of the officeholders who would not vote for the measure in May 2013 have changed their minds at the time this book went to press.

At Chick-Fil-A, Business Is Good

In 2012 when the fast-food chicken restaurant chain, Chick-Fil-A, found itself at the center of the gay marriage debate, some predicted the company's future could be in peril. Dan Cathy, Chick-Fil-A's CEO, stated in an interview that he believed marriage was between a man and a woman, setting off a national boycott by gay activists.

But the fast-food giant's revenues have grown immensely. Chick-Fil-A ended 2012 with $4.6 billion in sales – up 14 percent from the year before. The privately-owned company also opened 96 new stores, four more than in 2011.[205]

Imagine the national media coverage the company would have received had its sales diminished. Because the news was good, media had little to say.

Not All in LGBT Community Support Gay Marriage

Doug Mainwaring, co-founder of the National Capital Tea Party Patriots, published a commentary about why he is opposed to same-sex marriage on The Witherspoon Institute's Public Discourse website in March 2013. What makes Mainwaring's position newsworthy is the fact that he is a politically active gay man.[206] The same way the media will highlight Republicans who support gay marriage because it is outside the norm, a gay man who opposes gay marriage is equally outside the norm. However, Mainwaring rarely receives national media attention and is viewed as an enemy for many in the LGBT community.

"I wholeheartedly support civil unions for gays and lesbians, but I am opposed to same-sex marriage," he wrote. "Because activists have made marriage, rather than civil unions, their goal, I am viewed by many as a self-loathing, traitorous gay. So be it. I prefer to think of myself as a reasoning, intellectually honest human being."[207]

Mainwaring confirms the media's bias against anyone opposed to gay marriage. "Opposition to same-sex marriage is characterized in the media, at best, as clinging to 'old-fashioned' religious beliefs and traditions, and at worst, as homophobia and hatred."[208]

Mainwaring realized he was attracted to the same sex at about age 8 but, as an adult, entered into a heterosexual marriage to his "soul mate," who he met while singing in a youth choir. Mainwaring and his wife were unable to conceive and adopted two boys, but their marriage ended a few years later. Following the divorce, Mainwaring lived a largely homosexual lifestyle, but realized that his children needed a mother and a father.

"Over several years, intellectual honesty led me to some unexpected conclusions: 1) Creating a family with another man is not completely equal to creating a family with a woman, and 2) Denying children parents of both genders at home in an objective evil. Kids need and yearn for both."[209]

Ten years after the divorce, Mainwaring and his ex-wife decided to pull their family back together and live under one roof. Because of his predilections, they deny their own sexual impulses, but are closer than ever before.

"Moms and dads interact differently with their children," wrote Mainwaring. "To be fully formed, children need to be free to generously receive from and express affection to parents of both genders. Genderless marriages deny this fullness."[210]

Same-Sex Underage Relationship in Florida

In addition to the omission of political and business news that was not favorable for gay-marriage advocates, the national media also failed to highlight stories which included crimes committed by gay individuals. Yet, crimes *against* gays and lesbians are provided with widespread media coverage, because these actions support the narrative that gays and lesbians are perpetual victims.

The instance of an 18-year-old female high school student who engaged in a same-sex relationship with a 14-year-old classmate in Sebastian, Fla., is an example of the national media's knee-jerk reaction to any negative coverage about LGBT causes. Under normal circumstances, news of an 18-year-old having a sexual relationship with a 14-year-old would be covered as a horrendous crime. But with a lesbian female, Kaitlyn Hunt, involved as the aggressor, media representatives went to great lengths to paint her as a victim.

The campaign to exonerate Hunt shifted into high gear. At the press conference she held with her parents, Hunt wore a "Stop the Hate" t-shirt. Her mother, Kelly Hunt Smith, created a

Facebook page to gain support, and the page garnered over 46,000 members. Her father, Steven Hunt, set up a similar petition on Change.org calling for prosecutors to drop the charges. More than 300,000 people signed the petition. Steven Hunt claimed his daughter's relationship with the 14-year-old girl was consensual, and that the minor's parents went to the police only because his daughter was homosexual, ignoring the fact that a 14-year-old cannot consent to a sexual relationship with an adult.[211]

The parents of the 14-year-old, however, said on a television interview that they repeatedly asked Hunt to stop contact with their daughter, but the 18-year-old refused. As a result, the parents believed they had no choice but to file charges against Hunt. "We had no other alternative but to turn to the law, use it basically as a last resort," Jim Smith, the victim's father, told CNN.[212]

National media outlets offered no criticism of Kaitlyn Hunt whatsoever. "LGBT Injustice" was the headline used on the May 22, 2013 segment of MSNBC's "All In With Chris Hayes," where the host interviewed Hunt, her mother and their attorney. Hayes was completely sympathetic with Hunt, ignoring the fact that there was a victim in the case. He seemed to be more concerned about the "media firestorm" the high school senior was going through than the well-being of the 14-year-old she assaulted.

After Hunt was expelled from Sebastian River High School and charged with two counts of lewd and lascivious battery of a child, Hayes asserted that she was being singled out only because she was a lesbian and said he hoped that "common sense will prevail." If the perpetrator had been an 18-year-old male, especially a black male, there would be no question as to what action prosecutors should take. Yet, Hayes and a throng of gay activists actually expected the charges to be dropped. Bruce Colton, the state attorney for Florida's judicial circuit, offered Hunt's defense team two plea deals, both of which they refused to accept.[213]

Hayes and his media cohorts had the equivalent of egg on their faces a few months later when it was discovered that, despite the judge's ruling that there be no communication between Hunt and the 14-year-old until the trial occurred, Hunt had sent thousands of text messages, explicit videos and nude pictures to her underage friend. Apparently, Hunt had given the victim an iPod so they could exchange text messages. On Aug. 21, 2013, Judge Robert Pegg sent Hunt, then 19, to jail, ordering her held on bond pending trial, stating, "She simply can't be trusted to abide by the court order." The original charges against Hunt carry a maximum of 15 years in prison upon conviction.[214]

A public mea culpa by Hayes and other national media representatives who immediately leapt to Hunt's defense was appropriate and in order. But, to date, none has been forthcoming.

Gay Connecticut Couple Accused of Raping Adopted Children

George Harasz and Douglas Wirth, a married couple from Glastonbury, Conn., were arrested in November 2011 following allegations by two of their nine adopted children of sexual abuse.

The boys were 5 and 15 years old at the time. The warrants for the couple's arrest allege that the boys were touched inappropriately, sexually assaulted and physically abused. Some of the alleged abuse included forced labor, beatings, being physically restrained and being forced to sleep in closets.[215]

Harasz and Wirth adopted nine boys through the Department of Children and Families beginning in 2000. They received two waivers from DCF to exceed the limit for adopted children in one household, first in 2006 and then in 2008. The boys were removed from Harasz and Wirth's home after the investigation began in February 2011. As of the publication date of this book, the two men were still awaiting trial.[216]

National media representatives make decisions on a daily basis about which stories they will feature and which ones they will bury, never to see the light of day. Clearly, major stories that reflect a victory for proponents of traditional marriage, or which show members of the LGBT community in a negative light, are omitted, and it appears that the omission is likely intentional.

CHAPTER 11
PLAYING THE NUMBERS GAME

Another example of the media's complicity in promoting gay marriage is their tendency to allow gay activists to throw out bogus numbers regarding the magnitude and size of the gay population, and grossly exaggerate its impact on the overall American society. These numbers are presented during interviews and in news articles, unchallenged by the media, allowing the public to believe they are accurate when, in many cases, they are completely false.

In Chapter 5, I presented the example that 10 percent of the U.S. population is homosexual, a figure which is not supported by any empirical evidence. In fact, the percentage is about a third as large, or 3 percent, according to recent studies. But there are several other examples.

On MSNBC in March 2013, Aisha Moodie-Mills, a gay activist with the Center for American Progress, made the following statement: "Two million children are being raised by gays and lesbians." The host, Craig Melvin, did not challenge her statement, accepting it on its merits.

In fact, according to the U. S. Census Bureau, the number of same-sex couple households with children in the U.S. is only 115,064.[217] The National Center for Marriage and Family

Research estimates are even lower at 98,600.[218] With an average of two children per household, the total number of children being raised by gays and lesbians would then be somewhere between 190,000 and 230,000 – a far cry from the 2 million children Ms. Moodie-Mills claimed.

The Human Rights Campaign (HRC) estimates married gay couples miss out on over 1,000 federal rights, benefits and protections on account of DOMA, including the ability to collect a deceased spouse's Social Security benefits.[219] Have media asked the HRC to enumerate or produce the list of 1,000 benefits? No, instead members of the media merely repeat the statement without requesting any evidence of what these benefits are. Married couples who file Federal tax returns might be interested in exactly what benefits they are receiving. In some instances, a couple can actually pay fewer Federal taxes if they file separate returns, so the idea that those who are married always have an advantage is questionable.

During the debates leading up to the Supreme Court's decision in June 2013, several exaggerated claims were made. Gay activists boasted that over 100 Republican leaders signed an amicus brief in support of same-sex marriage, but they neglected to mention that only two out of the 100 were then currently elected officials. Instead, they let the public assume that the "Republican leaders" were all existing officeholders.[220]

LGBT activists also bragged that some NFL players had submitted a similar amicus brief. But with 32 NFL teams, each with 53 players on the active roster (totaling 1,696), those signing the brief amounted to less than one-fourth of 1 percent of all NFL players.[221]

Forty percent of homeless youth are gays or lesbians, according to LGBT activists. Their proof? A web-based survey conducted from October 2011 through March 2012 that included only 381 respondents, representing 354 agencies that work with homeless youth throughout the U.S. LGBT youth comprise approximately 40 percent of the clientele served by the agencies that responded to the survey.[222] From this limited data, gay activists draw the sweeping conclusion that 40 percent of *all* homeless youth are gays or lesbians.

Not only are web-based surveys notoriously unscientific, but the agencies that responded provide services to a limited segment of the American population. And the absence of any religious-based agencies included in the survey further skews the results. By the way, the survey was financed by several gay-oriented organizations -- The Palette Fund, True Colors Fund and the Williams Institute.

Promises of Economic Bonanza for States

The latest tactic used by gay activists is to assert that the legalization of gay marriage will be an economic boon for state and local economies. In other words, if LGBT advocates cannot persuade lawmakers to vote for gay marriage on the basis of perceived fairness or equity, perhaps these legislators can be coaxed by promises of additional funds for their state's coffers.

Time magazine interviewed a planner of gay weddings, Scott Stevens, owner of iowasgayweddingplanner.com, who said that his business had doubled since the Supreme Court struck down the Defense of Marriage Act (DOMA), and that 75 percent of his clients are from out of state.[223] But since Stevens specializes in gay weddings, an increase in business after the DOMA ruling is hardly earth-shattering news.

Richard D. Mohr, professor emeritus at the University of Illinois, wrote an opinion piece in August 2013 arguing that converting Illinois' civil union arrangements to marriages would retain thousands of dollars in the state through money saved in federal estate taxes paid to the federal government.[224] Mohr calculated a fiscal increase from weddings between in-state residents. This is not added money to the economy, it is merely redirecting cash. The only increase to the state budget would come from out-of-state residents.[225]

Others, like Angeliki Kastanis of Delaware, estimate that their states will experience a boost in spending in the wedding and tourism industries because of the numbers of gay weddings.

But the methods used to reach this conclusion are based on unrealistic and unverifiable assumptions. For example, Kastanis says that, according to the 2010 Census, 2,646 same-sex couples live in Delaware. She then surmises that 50 percent of those couples will get marriage licenses within the first three years after the passage of marriage equality.[226] Yet, studies have already shown that only about 20 percent of same-sex couples actually get married once their states pass gay marriage legislation. With data that is so glaringly inaccurate, how could an estimate of potential revenue be reliable?

Also, the estimates assume that the majority of same-sex couples who get married will have large weddings. After gay marriage was passed in several states, the media presented long lines of gay couples getting married at city halls. These were small, private ceremonies for which, presumably, little money was spent, with the exception of wedding rings and clothing for the occasion. Yes, newlyweds spent an average of $28,427 on weddings and related events in 2012.[227] But one cannot then conclude that all couples who get married spend that amount. Only those who have the income (or borrowing ability) to spend that amount will do so and the percentage of those who do is going to be relatively small.

Finally, should a legislator vote to legalize a practice that he believes is morally wrong simply because doing so will bring money to his state? If so, why not legalize prostitution? And many states do not have legalized gambling precisely because they believe that doing so will do more harm than good, even with the economic benefits.

The national media have a penchant for repeating whatever numbers gay advocates champion, apparently, without asking questions or checking the facts. As a result, consumers are fed a lot of information that is patently false or, at best, misleading. Must fact checkers take a hiatus when reports on the LGBT community are broadcast or published?

CHAPTER 12
WE ONLY REPORT POLL RESULTS THAT WE LIKE...

Polls regarding attitudes about gay marriage are conducted on a regular basis at both the state and national levels. The American public is constantly being told by the media that a majority of Americans are in favor of gay marriage, although that is not necessarily true. It depends upon which segment of the populace or region of the country is polled, as well as how the question is asked. In Chapter 2, I described how the results are substantially different when the question is asked regarding whether or not gay marriage should be legal, versus how marriage should be defined. Even so, it is a narrow, not an overwhelming majority of Americans who say they favor gay marriage when polled.

The reporting of polls can affect the outcome of future polls as the bandwagon effect takes hold. People want to support what is popular and, if gay marriage is viewed as popular, they may respond favorably, even if their genuine opinion has not changed.

Primarily, national media outlets report only the poll results that are favorable to gay causes and gay marriage, leaving the perception that the trend is widespread and irreversible. At the same time, they downplay or completely exclude poll results which indicate otherwise.

In March 2013, the *Washington Post* released a national poll showing that 58 percent of Americans supported gay marriage. Media outlets trumpeted these findings with sensational headlines, like that published on the ABC News website: "Poll Tracks Dramatic Rise In Support for Gay Marriage."[228]

The support in this poll was substantially higher than results previously obtained, and no other poll since then has come close to matching this percentage. Ordinarily, this should have led media representatives to view the results with skepticism. Yet, journalists' traditional roles as skeptics seem to be completely abandoned when reporting on gay activists' issues.

MSNBC's Chris Matthews announced the results with enthusiasm, although the numbers from polls released the week before had been much lower. In fact, two polls released the same day had a significantly lower percentage of support, which meant that the *Post*'s poll was clearly an outlier. But Matthews completely ignored the other polls during his "Hardball" broadcast, leaving his audience with the impression that support had jumped 5 percentage points in only a few days.

Instead, viewers are constantly told by the media that gay marriage nationwide is "inevitable." After the Supreme Court's ruling to strike down DOMA, media would interview a guest who was opposed to gay marriage and constantly tell them that they were fighting a lost cause because the polls showed Americans favor gay marriage. In other words, the media's message is that those who believe in traditional marriage should simply give up because they have no chance of winning the fight. Or expressed another way, media representatives give those who believe in traditional marriage the impression that, because gay marriage is "popular," they should support it.

On June 27, 2013, CNN's Wolf Blitzer interviewed Congressman Tim Huelskamp (R-Kan.) about a Constitutional amendment he was sponsoring that would ban gay marriage nationwide. Rather than focus his inquiries on the elements or purpose of the amendment during the three-minute interview, Blitzer instead told Huelskamp four different times that polls favored gay marriage so his amendment had virtually no chance of succeeding.

It is not the media's job to discourage, or encourage, individuals engaged in political movements. Their job is to objectively glean the information at hand and present it to consumers in an unbiased fashion.

As mentioned in previous sections of this book, polls show mixed results depending upon the question that is asked. When asked the question of the definition of marriage, more people support the traditional male/female model than the same-sex one. And the fact is that 38 states have amendments or referenda banning gay marriage. Just because voters in New York and California strongly support the practice, does not mean that the entire country will follow suit, or that it should.

How Americans Feel About Religious Beliefs and Commerce

In July 2013, Rasmussen released a poll that asked Americans if a business owner's religious beliefs could be taken into account when the entrepreneur considered accepting business from potential patrons. The question was worded thusly: Suppose a Christian wedding photographer has deeply held religious beliefs opposing same-sex marriage. If asked to work a same-sex wedding ceremony, should that wedding photographer have the right to say no? Eighty-five percent of American adults who responded believe the photographer has the right to say no. Only 8 percent disagreed. But national media representatives seemed to treat this poll as one of their best kept secrets.[229]

In August 2013, Michigan voters were asked whether they *opposed* legislation or a ballot measure seeking to allow same-sex marriage in the state, and a majority – 51 percent – said yes. The poll, conducted by Denno Research for the Lambert Edwards & Associates public relations firm, was largely ignored by the national media.[230]

Another tactic media use regarding reports about polls is to provide incomplete information regarding the source of the polls. On July 11, 2013, MSNBC's Chuck Todd released poll results in Virginia. Although the poll was conducted by a bipartisan team of pollsters, it was commissioned by the Human Rights Campaign (HRC), the largest and most influential lobbying organization for gay issues in the nation, which meant that there was an obvious built-in bias.

Whenever MSNBC or other media outlets release polling results that are commissioned by conservative-leaning organizations, such as the Rasmussen poll, they always include a disclaimer to that effect. Not so with this HRC poll, as Todd informed viewers that HRC's poll was "worth taking a look at."

Further, Todd failed to mention the poll's relatively small sample size of 600 respondents with a high margin of error of plus or minus 4.9 percentage points.[231] Todd also omitted the fact that the HRC's results were clearly an outlier, since its results were quite different from other polls taken in Virginia within the previous twelve months. A poll conducted in May 2013 by the University of Mary Washington's Center for Leadership and Media Studies showed Virginians were essentially split on the issue, with 46 percent opposed and 45 percent in support of same-sex marriage.[232]

In addition, since an overwhelming majority of Virginians voted for a constitutional amendment to define marriage as between one man and one woman, asking people if they are in favor of overturning the amendment might be a more appropriate question. I suspect, however, that, in asking that question, pollsters may not like the survey results.

Media will often emphasize the difference in generational support for gay marriage, citing the strong support among individuals under the age of 30. In doing so, they assume that young people will maintain their support for gay marriage in perpetuity. Yet, young people traditionally have much more liberal social views than their parents, but become more socially conservative as they age and gain more wisdom and experience. In other words, the fact that most young people support gay marriage now does not necessarily mean they always will in the future.

In addition, does the fact that polls show a large majority of young people support gay marriage translate into them being single issue voters? Does it mean that they will vote for or against a candidate for office based on that issue alone? The majority of young voters probably support legalizing marijuana too. Does that mean it should be legalized nationwide? Does it mean that adults who are older and have more life experience should make no attempt to give the young the benefit of their knowledge?

In fact, once today's youth mature and understand the consequences of having significant numbers of children raised without an identifiable mother or a father, they may begin to see the entire issue in a different light. Traditional marriage advocates Andrew Walker and Ryan Anderson, both of whom are Millennials, born during the Reagan administration, penned a heartfelt article explaining the importance of traditional marriage in child rearing. "Redefining marriage would further distance it from the needs of children and deny, as a matter of policy, the ideal that children need a mother and a father," they wrote in a May 21, 2013 commentary titled, "Refusing to Stay Silent: A Millennial Case for Marriage."[233]

Walker and Anderson also argue that redefining marriage would further marginalize traditional views and erode religious liberty. "Believing what virtually every human society believed until the past decade or so – that marriage is the union of a man and a woman ordered to procreation and family life," they wrote, "increasingly would be seen as a malicious prejudice to be driven to the margins of culture."

Finally, media make the unspoken assumption that poll numbers regarding gay marriage cannot change; that in whatever direction current polls are trending, the favorable numbers will grow into eternity. Yet, poll numbers changed in France. A survey published on May 26, 2013 showed support for gay marriage in France had plunged 10 percent, to 53 percent, in only six months. Gay marriage in France became legal in April 2013.[234]

CHAPTER 13
HELP FROM HOLLYWOOD

The news media play a pivotal role in the promotion of gay marriage, but they receive a tremendous amount of assistance from Hollywood in advocating homosexuality and gay marriage within popular culture. Nearly every television program – from sitcoms to dramas to reality TV to soap operas – features at least one character who is gay, lesbian, bisexual or transgendered, even though LGBT individuals represent only 3 percent of the population. Blacks and Hispanics represent 13 and 14 percent of the population respectively – more than four times the percentage of LGBT individuals. Yet neither black nor Hispanic characters have realized the same market penetration as far as television programming is concerned.

In this regard, Hollywood is simply an extension of the national media. Hollywood's mission appears to be to serve as the mind-control mechanism for the gay marriage movement. In the words of Rob Reiner, actor, movie producer and self-appointed gay marriage advocate, the effort has been an "education process." In Reiner's "Meet the Press" appearance on March 31, 2013, he did not pull any punches. "I believe there's an inevitability now. The snowball is rolling down the hill and it's inevitable."[235]

Presumably, by telling us all that gay marriage is inevitable, those of us who disagree will embrace defeat and acquiesce to the pressure exerted by gay activists. In other words, if they shout it loud enough and long enough, they seem to believe that the sheer volume of their words will overwhelm the opposition, even if their numbers cannot. Help from Hollywood further adds to the impression that the entire world, or at least the entire country, has embraced gay marriage, even though the facts do not support this notion.

This situation reminds me of the Biblical account of Caleb and Joshua. Twelve spies were sent by Moses into Canaan to explore whether or not the Promised Land was indeed habitable. When the spies returned, ten of them said that conquering the land was impossible.[236]

"And there we saw the giants, the sons of Anak, who come of the giants. And we were in our own sight, as grasshoppers, and so we were in their sight." But Caleb and Joshua, unwilling to embrace the "inevitability" of defeat, declared that the sons of Anak were not bigger than they were, and that the people should trust God and go into the land.[237]

Hollywood wants the American public to believe that gay activists and their supporters are like "giants," and that those who believe that traditional marriage is best for society are like "grasshoppers." But since 70 percent of Americans live in states where traditional marriage is still the law of the land, the balance of power remains with those who believe marriage is between a man and a woman, despite the tall tales told by Hollywood. Convictions, then, become the determining factor. The contingent that is most dedicated to its cause will ultimately be victorious.

Television Doesn't Influence Children, and Other Hollywood Malarkey

Gay activists argue that television has no influence on children and that the young will not be persuaded by homosexual imagery unless they already have a predetermined sexual orientation. This is an absurd notion. Multinational corporations spend billions of dollars every year on TV ads because they *know* television influences people's ideas, attitudes and behavior. And the virtual TV blackout of those who oppose gay marriage would be unnecessary if their opinions did not have the potential to influence the viewing audience.

Also, the debate about whether or not adult-oriented images affect children was settled long ago. The MPAA film rating system was implemented in November 1968 and rates movies based on their content, helping patrons decide which movies may be appropriate for children of different ages. It was established as an alternative to federal regulation of motion picture content by the U.S. government.[238]

Cable television providers followed suit and established channel blockers and parental controls in the 1990s. Gay activists cannot credibly argue that all television and film images have an impact on children *except* those which involve homosexuals.

In the 1990s, the television industry designed a TV ratings system to give parents more information about the content and age-appropriateness of TV programs. These ratings, called the

TV Parental Guidelines, were modeled after the familiar movie ratings, which parents have used as a guide for decades.[239] However, parents are at the mercy of the television industry regarding what it deems "appropriate" for children. Since Hollywood is so blatantly pro-gay, if their position is that gay intimacy and open discussions about homosexuality are "appropriate," the guidelines become meaningless. And if the industry views homosexual intimacy as mainstream, it's just a matter of time before it is included in children's programming, such as animated movies and cartoons.

The television rating "TV-MA-S" is actually equivalent to the X rating in films. Made-for-television films with this rating show sexual scenes with total frontal nudity, extended sexual intercourse, threesomes and gay and lesbian sex. Unfortunately, most parents are unaware of the meaning of this rating and, thus, may not realize that their children may be exposed to pornography through the monthly cable television service that is wired into their homes.

Cable networks were among the early proponents of homosexuality and gay programming, much of which focused on AIDS activism. With the smaller niche markets the stations reached, as opposed to the major networks, cable channels were less likely to offend a mass audience. MTV, with its reality show, "The Real World," first broadcast in 1992, pushed the envelope further and included gay characters as well as a gay wedding on one of its episodes.

"The Real World" focused on the lives of a group of strangers who auditioned to live together in a house for several months, as cameras recorded their interpersonal relationships. In the show's third season, the locale was San Francisco and one the housemates on the show was AIDS activist Pedro Zamora, one of the first openly gay men with AIDS to be portrayed in popular media.

Since MTV's audience was comprised almost exclusively of teenagers, its programming played a key role in desensitizing individuals who are now in their 30s with respect to homosexual intimacy. And unless parents actually watched the show, they had no idea about the images their teenage children were consuming.[240]

Within popular television programming, including sit-coms and dramatic one-hour shows, media portray anyone who is opposed to the promotion of homosexuality and gay marriage as either a redneck, a disingenuous opportunist, a closet homosexual or a religious zealot. And the pattern of a negative portrayal for those in opposition began years ago.

For example, a 1995 episode of the popular NBC television program, "Law and Order," titled "Pride," featured a politician pretending to be a right-wing, anti-gay bigot in order to kowtow to the prejudices of his constituents. The politician had murdered a gay city councilman, but the prosecutors were unable to convict him because of a hung jury.

Network television's promotion of homosexuality began mostly with comedic programming with a benign approach. The NBC show "Will and Grace," which ran from 1998 to 2006, featured two best friends who lived in New York. Will was a gay lawyer and Grace was a straight interior designer. The program also included a host of characters, some gay and some straight, who were Will's and Grace's friends, neighbors and business associates.

Since the mid-2000's, gay intimacy on television has become increasingly more graphic, even on programs targeted to a teen audience. On both ABC's "Glee" and CBS's "90210: The Next Generation," an updated version of the 1990s show "90210," gay characters kiss in the mouth and engage in sexual intimacy. NBC's "The New Normal," was a show launched in 2012 and featured a homosexual couple in the process of adopting a baby. However, the show was cancelled after only one season due to low ratings, protests from viewers, or both.[241] Presently, the instances of gay intimacy on television programs on nearly all cable and network channels are too numerous to count.

The Teen Nick network includes programming with gay and transgender characters, such as the program "DeGrassi." The industry has given "DeGrassi" a TV-PG rating, which stands for "parental guidance suggested." Yet, if parents associate movie ratings with television ratings, which many of them will, "PG" is often used for animated films and other movies for small children.

If parents prefer that their children not watch programs that put homosexuality front and center, parental controls will be ineffective as the industry has already given a green light to teen exposure to gay issues. A parent would not assume that homosexual characters and relationships would be necessarily included in a TV-PG-rated program. In fact, the opposite is probably true; they would assume that this subject matter and any matters concerning sexual relationships of any kind were *not* included.

Ben Shapiro, author of *Bullies: How the Left's Culture of Fear and Intimidation Silences America*, asserts that most major television shows are screened by the Gay and Lesbian Alliance Against Defamation (GLAAD) to ensure that they don't offend gay sensibilities. "Hollywood's been pushing gay marriage for years in its shows and movies – they actually see it as one of their great moral causes," he wrote.[242]

GLAAD makes no bones about its power and influence in the industry. On its website, the group describes itself as the leading organization that works directly with news media, entertainment media, cultural institutions and social media. The organization's mantra: "Leading the conversation. Shaping the media narrative. Changing the culture. That's GLAAD."[243]

Doug Mainwaring, a politically active gay man who was first introduced in Chapter 10 and opposes gay marriage, says the portrayal of gay life in shows like "Glee" or "Modern Family" is both inaccurate and incomplete.

"I find that men I know who have left their wives as they've come out of the closet often lead diminished, and in some cases nearly bankrupt, lives—socially, familially, emotionally and intellectually," he wrote. "They adjust their entire view of the world and their role within it in order to accommodate what has become the dominant aspect of their lives: their homosexuality. In doing so, they trade rich lives for one-dimensional lives."[244]

"Noah's Arc"

The cable television dramedy known as "Noah's Arc," is an example of television programming which mocks religion in general, and Christianity in particular. The program premiered in 2005 on the LOGO cable-television network, which is dedicated specifically to LGBT programming, and featured a cast of gay black and Latino characters. The show's content focused on LGBT issues, such as same-sex dating, same-sex marriage and parenthood, HIV and AIDS awareness, infidelity, promiscuity, and "homophobia."[245]

The producers of the program mock Christianity itself by their selection of a title that gay activists know has religious significance. The selection of this title, in and of itself, shows an utter disrespect for religion, and one can only conclude that the title was chosen specifically for that purpose.

Unsuspecting Christians who are channel surfing might accidentally tune in, believing that this program features the Biblical Noah who was instructed by God to build an ark in preparation of the onslaught of rain for 40 days and 40 nights. But they would be sorely mistaken as the title that lured them into its universe is the antithesis of what Noah had in mind. After all, Noah gathered all of the animals into the ark, two by two, male and female, to ensure that all species would continue to procreate and advance. In LOGO's "arc," only gay men are allowed.

Movies Also Have Major Impact

Hollywood's influence is hardly limited to television. Feature films depict gay characters in a generally positive light and, conversely, portray anyone who disagrees with gay marriage or opposes homosexuality on religious grounds as a kook, fanatic or religious zealot. The homophobic priest is a frequent character in Hollywood films dating back to the 1990s with "The Last Supper" and "The Wolves of Kromer," and, more recently, "Zombies of Mass Destruction" and "Pain and Gain."

The 2005 film "Brokeback Mountain" broke new ground by depicting two cowboys, characters who was usually considered to be extremely masculine, as two men in love with each other. "The entire purpose of the movie [was] to make homosexuality seem like something good and appealing, and to make people who are opposed to homosexuality bigots and homophobes," said David Kupelian, author of *The Marketing of Evil*, in an interview with *Charisma News*.[246]

Films will often subtly promote a political agenda which enthusiastically approves of gay marriage. In the film "Broken City," for example, the New York City mayor's wife (played by Katherine Zeta-Jones) gives a speech at a Human Rights Campaign event supporting gay marriage.

Without a doubt, Hollywood works hand-in-hand with the national media to promote gay marriage. Parents who genuinely care about the images to which their children are exposed must be extremely diligent in screening television programming in their homes. They cannot rely on Hollywood to use restraint when developing programming for teens and children, nor when deciding which ratings to apply.

CHAPTER 14
WHAT SHOULD THE AMERICAN PUBLIC DO?

Throughout this book, I've provided clear and convincing evidence that national media have a decided bias in favor of gay marriage. Absent tuning out national media altogether, which is not a viable option for those who like to be informed about current events, what should the American public do?

In a perfect world, we would be able to depend on national media to demonstrate some semblance of objectivity on the subject of gay marriage. Unfortunately, we are well beyond any hope of that.

The onus, then, is on the individual consumer to stay abreast of news on this front by casting a wider net and expanding the sources of information obtained. Fortunately, the Internet provides the opportunity to do so.

For news on the international front, Reuters, *The Guardian* and BBC tend to provide more objective worldwide reporting on the issue of gay marriage than does the American media. These are all British-based media outlets, and the point of view is not as strident as U.S. media. All three will still actually report balanced news that is not totally favorable to gay activists and gay marriage, and has a degree of objectivity.

The following news or organization web sites are also helpful:

- **American Family Association**: Non-profit organization on the "frontlines of America's culture war" since 1977 (www.afa.net)
- **Baptist Press**: News with a Christian perspective (www.bpnews.net)
- **Black Christian News Network**: The #1 daily black Christian Internet newspaper (www.bcnn1.com)
- **Charisma News**: Christian and under-reported secular news that concerns Christians. (www.charismanews.com)
- **Christian News:** Provides up-to-date news and information affecting the body of Christ worldwide from an uncompromising Biblical worldview (www.christiannews.net)
- **Christian Post**: The largest Christian newspaper in the world featuring world Christian news, Christian news sites, and religious news (www.christianpost.com)
- **ExMinistries:** Sheds light on the hip hop subculture (www.exministries.com)
- **Family Research Council:** Christian organization promoting the traditional family unit and the Judeo-Christian value system upon which it is built (www.frc.org)

- **Gay Christian Movement Watch**: Cutting-edge Christian ministry whose mission is to monitor, analyze and publish the activities, leaders and public theological positions of the "gay Christian movement" (www.gcmwatch.com)
- **Life Site News:** Portal of news stories about pro-life issues in Canada, the United States and the U.K. (www.lifesitenews.com)
- **National Organization for Marriage**: Non-profit advocacy organization for traditional marriage (www.nationformarriage.org)
- **One Million Moms**: Arm of the non-profit group, American Family Association, and stands "against the immorality, violence, vulgarity and profanity the entertainment media is throwing at your children" (www.onemillionmoms.com)
- **Parents and Friends of Ex-Gays and Gays**: Supports families, advocates for the ex-gay community, and educates the public on sexual orientation (www.pfox.org)
- **The Public Discourse**: Online publication of the Witherspoon Institute that seeks to enhance the public understanding of the moral foundations of free societies (www.thepublicdiscourse.com)

The above-listed websites or organizations advocate for traditional marriage. Since the national media unabashedly advocate for gay marriage, and if consumers regularly absorb national media, visiting these sites will provide them with a more balanced viewpoint.

Another step consumers can take is that, when they see imbalances in media coverage regarding gay marriage, contact the network, newspaper, magazine, or Website. They can send an email or letter to the media entity expressing concern about the other side not being heard. If media hear from enough people, they will be compelled to do a better job of providing more even-handed coverage. If they do not hear from the public, they will assume that viewers are satisfied with the news presentations and will continue business as usual.

No matter what decision you ultimately make, if you care about traditional marriage and the future of American society, sitting on the sidelines is no longer an option. Getting involved is the only way to effect change.

CHAPTER 15
WHAT COMES NEXT?

Based on the slanted and one-sided coverage national media present, it is clear that they are almost unanimously in favor of gay marriage. They believe it should be legalized in all 50 states, and that anyone who does not agree is motivated by bigotry, ignorance or animus. They also believe that anyone who does not approve of gay marriage should pay a price, either politically, economically, professionally, or all three.

But that is not a decision the national media can or should make for the American public. It is not the media's responsibility to persuade the public in a particular political direction. They do not have the right to shove the latest social trends down the collective throats of the American people. It is not their right to infringe on the religious freedoms granted to American citizens by the U.S. Constitution. Their charge is to present the information to the public and let Americans make up their own minds.

The American consumer has been conditioned to believe that the media report the truth, and that journalists are simply portraying American attitudes about gay marriage and other issues as they actually exist. After reading this book, I hope consumers clearly understand that media are doing just the opposite. I also hope that consumers will begin to be more analytical regarding the media's obvious bias regarding this issue, and that they will begin demanding better from what is known as the "Fourth Estate."

Is there any hope for compromise on the issue of gay marriage? Years ago, there might have been. But I believe we are well past that point. Those of us who believe that it is simply too risky a proposition to tinker with an institution that has been the foundation of society since time immemorial are not likely to change our minds. Whether motivated by religious beliefs, moral convictions, or common sense, to abandon our principles is simply not an option.

Gay activists like to present this issue in micro terms: Harry and Jim (or Betsy and Jane) love each other and want to get married. What could be the harm of that, they ask. Yet, for those who believe in traditional marriage, the issue is much larger than Harry, Jim, Betsy and Jane. Once the Pandora's box of marriage re-definition is opened, everything around us will be affected.

The macro effect will be enormous as the minds of the young are re-programmed to no longer believe in traditional family structures or view them as important. The offspring – the children who are born within the ensuing loosely formed, transitional households – will suffer most. Government agencies, school systems, neighborhoods and, in some cases, the criminal justice system will be expected to step into the breach. The pressures on the social safety net will be tremendous.

Furthermore, the push for gay marriage will not end the demands of gay activists, even if nationwide legalization is realized. Efforts to up the ante will continually occur. Ellen Sturtz, a gay activist who confronted First Lady Michelle Obama at a Democratic National Committee fundraiser in June 2013, wrote that her contributions to President Obama's election coffers were made with an expectation that an executive order benefitting LGBT individuals would be signed.

"Millions of LGBT Americans continue to experience the enormous pain of living and working in the closet, not allowed to acknowledge who we are and who we love," she wrote in a *Washington Post* op-ed piece.[247] In other words, she and other activists will not be satisfied until all LGBT individuals feel comfortable coming out of the closet, an eventuality that is nearly impossible to be realized. Meanwhile, those who view the world differently are expected to roll over and play dead or, at the very least, be muzzled by the media. We are expected to remain silent and let gay activists be the only ones allowed to have an opinion, regardless of the foreseeable harm done as a result of their demands.

At the same time that they acknowledge that only a slight majority of Americans favor gay marriage, gay activists insist that those who disagree be banished from the airwaves. "But even today, anti-LGBT activists, who continue to wrongfully state that gay people are unfit to be parents, have a platform in the media to spread their lies," wrote Dave Montez and Wilson Cruz in *The Atlantic* magazine. "We have a long way to go before groups like the National Organization for Marriage are no longer routinely invited to provide 'balance' on national cable news program."[248] For Montez, Cruz and other gay activists, only a complete exclusion from the media of voices who believe in traditional marriage will suffice. No need for media 'balance' is necessary.

My expectation is that members of the media and gay activists will attack this book and dismiss it in a sweeping fashion. But facts cannot be easily dismissed and I took special care to ensure that my research and documentation were rock solid. One thing about the truth is that it always eventually surfaces. My heart's desire for the readers of this book can be found in John 8:32 in the New Testament: "Ye shall know the truth and the truth shall set you free."

ABOUT THE AUTHOR

Gwen Richardson has been a political writer and observer for more than 20 years. Her commentaries have appeared in several daily newspapers, including the *Houston Chronicle, Detroit Free Press, Dallas Morning News* and *Philadelphia Inquirer*. In the 1990s, she was a monthly columnist for *USA Today*, and editor of *Headway* magazine, a monthly public affairs publication. A long-time entrepreneur and a graduate of Georgetown University, Ms. Richardson currently resides in Houston, Texas. This is her fourth published book.

Communication via email is welcome. Email the author at gwenrichardson123@gmail.com.

OTHER BOOKS BY GWEN RICHARDSON
(Kindle version also available)

The Genesis Files is a fast-paced mystery based in Houston, Texas. The main character is a journalist, Lloyd Palmer, who meets a mysterious stranger while interviewing potential witnesses to a murder-suicide. This chance meeting leads Lloyd down a path which changes his life, but his journey is fraught with peril, as both he and his family barely escape a hired assassin. 312 pp. $15.00

Write It Right: The Guide to Self-Publishing Your Best Book provides both aspiring and seasoned authors with a road map to success. 142 pp. $12.00

Autographed copies of all titles by Gwen Richardson can be ordered via her web site: www.gwenrichardson.com

Copies can also be ordered by calling Cushcity Communications at its toll-free number: 1-800-340-5454

Other online sources for purchase: www.amazon.com and www.createspace.com

NOTES

INTRODUCTION

[1] "Poll: Attitudes Toward Gays Changing Fast," Dec. 5, 2012, Susan Page, *USA Today*, www.usatoday.com
[2] Paul Hitlin, Amy Mitchell and Mark Jurkowitz, "News Coverage Conveys Strong Momentum for Same-Sex Marriage," June 17, 2013, www.journalism.org.
[3] "Lesbians: Coming Out Strong/What Are the Limits of Intolerance," June 21, 1993, *Newsweek*.
[4] "Time Gay Marriage Cove: 'Gay Marriage Already Won,'" Jack Mirkinson, March 28, 2013, Huffington Post, www.huffingtonpost.com.
[5] "The Power List 2013," Out.com Editors, April 20, 2013, *Out* magazine, www.out.com
[6] "Report Calculates High Cost of Iraq/Afghanistan War," Kevin A. Hazlett, April 5, 2013, *Harvard Crimson*.
[7] Hitlin, Mitchell and Jurkowitz, 2013.

CHAPTER 1: HIJACKING THE CIVIL RIGHTS MOVEMENT

[8] Dr. Claud Anderson, *Black Labor, White Wealth*, 1994, PowerNomics Corporation of America, pp. 67-68.
[9] "Focus on the Slave Trade," Sept. 3, 2001, www.bbcnewsco.uk
[10] Jeninne Lee-St. John, "Viewpoint: Civil Rights and Gay Rights, *Time*, Oct. 25, 2005, www.time.com
[11] Donald Bogle, *Dorothy Dandridge: A Biography*, Amistad Press, p. 47, 1997.
[12] "After Being Fired for His Beliefs, Frank Turek Helps Other Marriage Supporters in Similar Position," Aug. 13, 2013, National Organization for Marriage, www.nomblog.com
[13] Brenda Howard, "I left my job over a computer-desktop hoodie," Aug. 16, 2013, *The Washington Post*, www.washingtonpost.com
[14] Howard, 2013.
[15] Howard, 2013.
[16] Ellen Sturtz, "Why I confronted the first lady," June 7, 2013, *The Washington Post*, www.washingtonpost.com
[17] Taylor Branch, *Parting the Waters: America in the King Years 1954-1963*, p. 273-274, Touchstone, 1988.
[18] Taylor Branch, p. 230, 1988.
[19] Taylor Branch, pp. 313-314, 1988.

[20] Taylor Branch, p. 328, 1988.
[21] Susan Meador Tobias, "My father's gay marriage," April 5, 2013, *The Washington Post*, www.washingtonpost.com
[22] Martin C. Evans, "Gay Marriage Gained Bush Black Votes," Nov. 14, 2004, *Newsday*.
[23] "Human Rights Campaign Contributions to Federal Candidates," www.opensecrets.org
[24] "Nationwide Poll of African American Adults," Zogby Analytics, February 2013.
[25] Rev. Osagyefo Uhuru Sekou, "Dear Marriage Equality Advocates: I Cannot Celebrate With You Today," June 26, 2013, www.newblackman.blogspot.com
[26] Elahe Izadi, "African-Americans, the Last Democratic Holdouts on Gay Marriage?" May 1, 2013, *National Journal*, www.nationaljournal.com
[27] Elahe Izadi, 2013.
[28] Pew Research Center for the People and the Press, "In Gay Marriage Debate, Both Supporters and Opponents See Legal Recognition as 'Inevitable'," June 6, 2013, www.people-press.org.
[29] Zogby Analytics, 2013.
[30] Izadi, 2013.
[31] Izadi, 2013.

CHAPTER 2: STACKING THE DECK

[32] Matt Hadro, "MRC Study: CNN Handed Airwaves to Liberals After Supreme Court Decisions," June 27, 2013, www.mrg.org.
[33] Jack Mirkinson, "Gay Journalists' Visibility During Supreme Court Coverage A Sign of A Changing Country," June 27, 2013, Huffington Post, www.huffingtonpost.com
[34] David Lauter, "Opposition to same-sex marriage increasingly isolated, pollsters say," March 7, 2013, *Los Angeles Times*, www.articles.latimes.com
[35] "Pope Francis on Gays: Who Am I To Judge?" July 29, 2013, CBS News, www.cbsnews.com
[36] Philip Pullella, "Pope Says Gays Should Not Be Marginalized," July 29, 2013, www.reuters.com
[37] Chris Cillizza and Sean Sullivan, "A majority of the country supports gay marriage. Will any 2016 Republican presidential candidate?" June 27, 2013, *The Washington Post*, www.washingtonpost.com
[38] Erik Wemple, "Media biased against traditional marriage, says

advocate," March 30, 2013, *The Washington Post*, www.washingtonpost.com.
[39] Diane Bullock, "Which Industries Stand to Benefit From Same-Sex Marriage?" Apr. 19, 2013, Minyanville, www.minyanville.com
[40] Wemple, 2013.
[41] Wemple, 2013.
[42] "Growing Support for Gay Marriage: Changed Minds and Changing Demographics," March 20, 2013, Pew Research Center for the People and the Press, www.people-press.org
[43] Hart/McInturff, "Study #13127, NBC News/Wall Street Journal Survey," April 2013, *The Wall Street Journal*, www.online.wsj.com
[44] Emily Swanson, "Marriage Equality Survey Finds Sharp Division Over DOMA Case," June 6, 2013, Huffington Post, www.huffingtonpost.com

CHAPTER 3: CARROTS AND STICKS

[45] Definition of "carrot and stick," www.dictionary.reference.com
[46] Tim Murphy and Dana Liebelson, "Which Politicians Supported Gay Marriage and When?" Mar 26, 2013, *Mother Jones*, www.motherjones.com
[47] Michael Catalini, "There Are Now Only 7 Senate Democrats Opposing Gay Marriage," May 30, 2013, *National Journal*, www.nationaljournal.com
[48] Andy Lewis, "Jason Collins: Agents Analyze Endorsement Potential," May 8, 2013, *Hollywood Reporter*, www.hollywoodreporter.com
[49] "Jason Collins given award by gay-straight alliance group," May 9, 2013, *USA Today*, www.usatoday.com
[50] Arlette Saenz, "Michelle Obama, Jason Collins Headline Fundraiser in New York City," May 30, 2013, ABC News, www.abcnews.go.com
[51] "World Pride Power List 2013: 100 Most Influential LGBT People Of the Year," June 28, 2013, *Guardian*, www.guardian.co.uk.
[52] Howard Beck, "Approval, but No New Team Yet, for Collins," *The New York Times*, July 8, 2013, www.nytimes.com
[53] Jason Collins with Franz Lidz, "Why NBA Center Jason Collins is coming out now," April 29, 2013, *Sports Illustrated*, www.si.com
[54] Jason Collins with Franz Lidz, 2013.
[55] Chris Chase, "Jason Collins' ex-fiancee tells her side of the story," July 8, 2013, *USA Today*, www.usatoday.com
[56] Chris Chase, 2013.
[57] Dylan Byers, "Daily Beast retracts Howie Kurtz post," May 2, 2013, *Politico*, www.politico.com.

58 Jeff Bercovici, "Howard Kurtz's Bad Reporting About Jason Collins Cost Him a Lot of Money," May 6, 2013, *Forbes*, www.forbes.com.
59 Out.com, 2013.
60 Tom McCarthy, "Howard Kurtz quits CNN to take up hosting job at Fox News," June 20, 2013, *Guardian*, www.guardian.co.uk
61 Jeff Zillgitt, "Roy Hibbert fined $75K for homophobic, vulgar remarks," June 2, 2013, *USA Today*, www.usatoday.com

CHAPTER 4: STICKS AND STONES MAY BREAK MY BONES. . .
62 Ryan T. Anderson, "Civility, Bullying and Same-Sex Marriage," July 15, 2013, The Heritage Foundation, www.heritage.org
63 Jeffrey Toobin, "Gay Marriage at the Supreme Court: Wedding Bells," April 1, 2013, *The New Yorker*, www.newyorker.com
64 "Religious Groups' Official Positions on Same-Sex Marriage," Dec. 7, 2012, www.pewforum.org
65 Adam Nossiter, "Senegal Cheers Its President for Standing Up to Obama on Same-Sex Marriage," June 28, 2013, *The New York Times*, www.nytimes.com
66 Mark Hemingway, "The Media's Double Standard: Some hate crimes are less hateful than others," Aug. 19, 2013, *The Weekly Standard*, www.weeklystandard.com

CHAPTER 5: PREVARICATION AND MENDACITY
67 "Notes and Queries," *Guardian*, www.guardian.co.uk
68 "By the Numbers: Same Sex Marriage," Caitlin Stark, March 26, 2013, CNN, www.cnn.com
69 "NBC News/Wall Street Journal Survey," Hart/McInturff, April 2013, MSNBC, www.msnbcmedia.msn.com
70 "USA's Shifting Attitudes Toward Gay Men and Lesbians," Susan Page, Dec. 5, 2012, *USA Today*, www.usatoday.com.
71 Wikipedia listing for Elizabeth Birch, www.wikipedia.org
72 Pew Research Center for the People and the Press, June 6, 2013.
73 Georgetown/On Faith, "President Obama on gay marriage rulings at Supreme Court: Churches can still define marriage how they wish," June 27, 2013, *The Washington Post*, www.washingtonpost.com
74 Jacob Gershman, "Photographers Discriminated Against Gay Couple, Court Rules," Aug. 22, 2013, *The Wall Street Journal*, www.blogs.wsj.com
75 Gershman, 2013.
76 Gershman, 2013.

77 The Supreme Court of the State of New Mexico, Elane Photography, LLC v. Vanessa Willock, Aug. 22, 2013, Docket Number 33,687, *The Wall Street Journal*, www.online.wsj.com

78 Denver CBS Local, "Lakewood Cake Shop Refuses Wedding Cake to Gay Couple," July 28, 2012, www.denver.cbslocal.com

79 "Commission Opposes T-Shirt Company's Refusal to Print 'Gay Pride' Message," Bethany Monk, Nov. 28, 2012, www.citizenlink.com

80 "Richland Florist Headed to Court Over Gay Marriage," April 10, 2013, *The News Tribune*, www.thenewstribune.com

81 Brian S. Brown, "Abraham Lincoln Would Approve of 'Marriage Equality'?!" Aug. 12, 2013, National Organization for Marriage, www.nomblog.com

82 "Gortz Haus objects to same-sex wedding," Aug. 8, 2013, *Des Moines Register*, www.desmoinesregister.com

83 "Same-Sex Marriage Law," Minnesota Department of Human Rights, www.mn.gov

84 Travis Loller, "Churches Changing Bylaws After Gay Marriage Ruling," Aug. 24, 2013, The Associated Press, www.hosted.ap.org

85 "Boy Scouts May lose state tax-exempt status in state as bill heads to vote," Aug. 28, 2013, *Long Beach Press Telegram*, www.presstelegram.com

86 Reuters Staff, "Dartmouth nixes hire of African bishop on past gay rights stance," Aug. 16, 2013, Reuters, www.blogs.reuters.com

87 Reuters Staff, 2013.

88 Reuters Staff, 2013.

89 "After Court, Gay Rights Spotlight Shifts Back to Obama," Jeff Mason, April 14, 2013, Reuters, www.reuters.com.

90 "Religious Groups Reap Federal Aid for Pet Projects," Diana B. Henriques and Andrew W. Lehren, May 13, 2007, *The New York Times*, www.nytimes.com.

91 Ibid.

92 "What War On Religion?," Stephanie Mencimer, Feb. 16, 2012, *Mother Jones*, www.motherjones.com.

93 "Canadian Supreme Court Rules Biblical Speech Opposing Homosexual Behavior is a 'Hate Crime,'" Heather Clark, Feb. 28, 2013, www.christiannews.net.

94 "Ecuadorean Preacher Fined $3,000, Banned From Politics for Calling Homosexuality 'Immoral,'" Heather Clark, March 14, 2013, www.christiannews.net

95 "Gay couple to sue church over gay marriage opt-out," Aug. 1, 2013,

www.christian.org.uk
[96] Sophia Charalambous, "Gay dads set to sue over church same-sex marriage opt-out," Aug. 2, 2013, *Essex Chronicle*, www.essexchronicle.co.uk
[97] Drew DeSilver, "Ahead of same-sex marriage decisions, what you need to know," June 21, 2013, Pew Research Center, www.pewresearch.org
[98] Jaweed Kaleem, "Religious Views Among Lesbian, Gay, Bisexual, Transgender People Revealed in New Survey," June 14, 2013, Huffington Post, www.huffingtonpost.com
[99] "Gay Marriage: Key Data Points From Pew Research," June 11, 2013, Pew Research Center, www.pewresearch.org
[100] Pew Research Center, 2013.
[101] Danny Hakim, "Exemptions Were Key to Vote on Gay Marriage," June 25, 2011, *The New York Times*, www.nytimes.com
[102] Anthony D. Romero Biography, American Civil Liberties Union, www.aclu.org

CHAPTER 6: ENDORSING THE "BORN THAT WAY" MYTH
[103] "Homosexual Orientation in Twins: A Report on 61 Pairs and Three Triplet Sets," Frederick Whitam, Ph.D., Milton Diamond, Ph.D., James Martin, B.A., Pacific Center for Sex and Society, 1993, www.hawaii.edu
[104] David France, "The Science of Gaydar," June 17, 2007, *The New Yorker*, www.nymag.com
[105] France, 2007.
[106] France, 2007.
[107] France, 2007.
[108] John H. McDonald, "Myths of Human Genetics: Hair Whorl," Dec. 8, 2011, University of Delaware, www.udel.edu
[109] McDonald, 2011.
[110] McDonald, 2011.
[111] Carol Moello, "Gays feel more accepted by still stigmatized, Pew Research Center survey finds," June 13, 2013, www.washingtonpost.com
[112] Meredith Goad, "Psychological Effects of Abuse," March 18, 2000, www.snapnetwork.org
[113] Nicola Menzie, "Pastor Donnie McClurkin 'Uninvited' From MLK Memorial Concert Over 'Ex-Gay' Testimony?" Aug. 12, 2013, *The Christian Post*, www.christianpost.com
[114] Rev. Clenard Childress, Jr., "Homosexual activists bully Donnie

McClurkin," Aug. 26, 2013, Black News, www.blacknews.com
[115] Gill Pringle, "Anne Heche Interview: 'There Is No Joy In My Family,'" May 1, 2011, www.telegraph.co.uk
[116] Janet Boynes, *Called Out: A Former Lesbian's Discovery of Freedom*, Creation House, Dec. 2008, p. 5
[117] Janet Boynes Ministry Website, www.janetboynesministries.com

CHAPTER 7: ENDORSING THE "IF YOU'RE GAY, YOU CAN'T CHANGE" MYTH

[118] R. Cort Kirkwood, "Former APA President Says Homosexuals Can Change," June 7, 2012, *The New American*, www.thenewamerican.com
[119] Matthew Cullinan Hoffman, "Former president of APA says organization controlled by 'gay rights' movement," June 4, 2012, *Life Site News*, www.lifesitenews.com
[120] "Letter in response to the closure of Exodus" International North America," July 2013, www.exoduslatinoamerica.com
[121] Stephanie Pappas and Tia Ghose, "Gay Conversion Therapy: What You Should Know," Aug. 19, 2013, *Live Science*, www.livescience.com
[122] "Judge rejects conversion therapy group's attempt to have SPLC case thrown out," July 19, 2013, Southern Poverty Law Center, www.splcenter.org
[123] Rosaria Champagne Butterfield and Tony Reinke, "From Radical Lesbian to Redeemed Christian: An Autobiographical Interview with Rosaria Champagne Butterfield," Feb. 18, 2013, Authors on the Line, www.desiringgod.org
[124] Aliyah Frumin, "8 things you may not know about Jeff Bezos," Aug. 6, 2013, MSNBC, www.tv.msnbc.com
[125] David Wilkins, Review of *Leaving Homosexuality: A Practical Guide for Men and Women Looking for a Way Out* by Alan Chambers, www.amazon.com
[126] Brittany T. Correa, Review of *Coming Out of Homosexuality: New Hope for Men and Women* by Bob Davies and Lori Rentzel, www.amazon.com
[127] "AC 360," CNN, Sept. 25, 2013.

CHAPTER 8: EVERYTHING'S COMING UP ROSES

[128] Charles C. W. Cooke, "The Gay Divorcees," May 15, 2012, *National Review*, www.nationalreview.com
[129] Doug Mainwaring, "Same-Sex Marriage Fever: Prohibition

Parallels," Apr. 15, 2013, *The Public Discourse*, www.thepublicdiscourse.com

[130] David Filipov, "5 years later, views shift subtly on gay marriage," Nov. 17, 2008, *Boston Globe*, www.boston.com

[131] Commonwealth of Massachusetts, Registry of Vital Records and Statistics, June 24, 2013.

[132] Commonwealth of Massachusetts, 2013.

[133] Cooke, 2012.

[134] Cooke, 2012.

[135] Ezra Klein, "Scalia's gay adoption claim: Even wronger than I thought," March 29, 2013, *The Washington Post*, www.washingtonpost.com

[136] Mark Regnerus, "How different are the adult children of parents who have same-sex relationships? Findings from the New Family Structures Study," March 12, 2012, *Social Science Research*, www.elsevier.com

[137] Ana Samuel, "The Kids Aren't All Right: New Family Structures and the 'No Differences' Claim," June 14, 2012, *The Public Discourse*, www.thepublicdiscourse.com

[138] Regnerus, 2012.

[139] Kathleen Doheny, "Divorce in Early Childhood May Harm Adult ties With Parents: Study," July 16, 2013, *U.S. News*, www.health.usnews.com

[140] Peter Jon Mitchell, "Parents, the first educators," Oct. 28, 2009, Mercatornet, www.mercatornet.com

[141] Robert Oscar Lopez, "Growing Up With Two Moms: The Untold Children's View," Aug. 6, 2012, *The Public Discourse*, www.thepublicdiscourse.com

[142] Lopez, 2012.

[143] Lopez, 2012.

[144] Samuel, 2012.

[145] Lopez, 2012.

[146] Samuel, 2012.

[147] Samuel, 2012.

[148] Eric Metaxas, "First-Person: Wanting a mom and dad – the children of same-sex couples," June 4, 2013, *Baptist Press*, www.baptistpress.com

[149] Lopez, 2012.

[150] Karen Clark and Elizabeth Marquardt, "The Sperm-Donor Kids Are Not Really all Right," June 14, 2010, *Slate*, www.slate.com

[151] Clark and Marquardt, 2010.
[152] Clark and Marquardt, 2010.
[153] Clark and Marquardt, 2010.
[154] Clark and Marquardt, 2010.
[155] Kathleen Parker, "Surrogacy exposed," May 24, 2013, *The Washington Post*, www.washingtonpost.com
[156] Parker, 2013.
[157] Parker, 2013.
[158] "Who Is At Risk for HIV Infection and Which Populations Are Most Affected?" July 2012, National Institute on Drug Abuse, www.drugabuse.gov
[159] David E. Beck M.D. and Mark L. Welton M.D., " Bacterial Sexually Transmitted Diseases," November 2004, National Institutes of Health, www.ncbi.nlm.nih.gov
[160] Hyun-Jun Kim and Karen I. Fredriksen-Goldsen, PhD, "Hispanic Lesbians and Bisexual Women at Heightened Risk or Health Disparities," July 11, 2011, *American Journal of Public Health*, www.ajph.aphapublications.org
[161] Mark S. Friedman, Michael P. Marshal, et al, "A Meta-Analysis of Disparities in Childhood Sexual Abuse, Parental Physical Abuse, and Peer Victimization Among Sexual Minority and Sexual Nonminority Individuals," June 20, 2010, *American Journal of Public Health*, www.ajph.aphapublications.org
[162] Karen I. Fredriksen-Goldsen, Hyun-Jun Kim, and Susan E. Barkan, "Disability Among Lesbian, Gay and Bisexual Adults: Disparities in Prevalance and Risk," July 12, 2011, *American Journal of Public Health*, www.ajph.aphapublications.org
[163] Andrea L. Roberts, Margaret Rosario, et al, "Elevated Risk of Posttraumatic Stress in Sexual Minority Youths: Mediation by Childhood Abuse and Gender Nonconformity," Oct. 6, 2011, *American Journal of Public Health*, www.ajph.aphapublications.org
[164] Trista A. Bingham, Nina T. Harawa, and John K. Williams, "Gender Role Conflict Among African American Men Who Have Sex With Men and Women: Associations With Mental Health and Sexual Risk and Disclosure Behaviors," Apr. 6, 2012, *American Journal of Public Health*, www.ajph.aphapublications.org
[165] Samuel, 2012.
[166] Liza Mundy, "The Gay Guide to Wedded Bliss," May 22, 2013, *The Atlantic*, www.theatlantic.com
[167] Mundy, 2013.

168 Mundy, 2013.
169 Mundy, 2013.
170 Mundy, 2013.
171 Commonwealth of Massachusetts, 2013.
172 Mundy, 2013.
173 Mundy, 2013.
174 Ryan T. Anderson, "The Social Costs of Abandoning the Meaning of Marriage," Sept. 9, 2013, The Heritage Foundation, www.heritage.org
175 Showtime website, www.sho.com/sho/polyamory-married-and-dating/about, Accessed Sept. 21, 2013.
176 Molly Young, "He & He & He," June 29, 2012, New York, www.nymag.com
177 Young, 2012.
178 Paul Rampell, "A high divorce rate means it's time to try 'wedleases'," Aug. 4, 2013, The Washington Post, www.washingtonpost.com

CHAPTER 9: SEE NO EVIL, HEAR NO EVIL

179 Ben Shapiro, "The Gay Marriage Bullies," Blog Post, Feb. 28, 2013, www.bclabjfoley.blogspot.com
180 Rachel Abramowitz, "Film fest director resigns," Nov. 26, 2008, Los Angeles Times, www.articles.latimes.com
181 Abramowitz, 2008.
182 Jesse McKinley, "Theater Director Resigns Amid Gay-Rights Ire," Nov. 13, 2008, The New York Times, www.theater.nytimes.com
183 Steve Lopez, "Prop 8 stance upends her life," Dec. 14, 2008, Los Angeles Times, www.articles.latimes.com
184 Lopez, 2008.
185 Ben Johnson, "'Angry Queers' smash church windows in Portland," Apr. 26, 2012, Life Site News, www.lifesitenews.com
186 Johnson, 2012.
187 "2013 LGBT community survey results: Starbucks does well, Chick-fil-A doesn't," Aug. 27, 2013, Wisconsin Gazette, www.wisconsingazette.com
188 Karlene Lukovitz, "QSR Top 50: Chick-fil-a Surpasses KFC in 2012 Sales," Aug. 1, 2013, Marketing Daily, www.mediapost.com
189 Carol Cratty and Michael Pearson, "DC shooter wanted to kill as many as possible, prosecutors say," Feb. 7, 2013, CNN, www.cnn.com
190 Cratty and Pearson, 2013.
191 "Enfield Man Admits Mailing Threats," August 22, 2012, CBS

Connecticut, www.connecticut.cbslocal.com
[192] Kirsten Andersen, "Homosexual activist who sent death threats sentenced to five years' probation," Apr. 17, 2013, *Life Site News*, www.lifesitenews.com
[193] "Belgian bishops criticize women's water attack on archbishop," April 26, 2013, Catholic News Service, www.catholicregister.org
[194] "Preacher Attacked at Seattle Gay Pridefest 2013," www.YouTube.com
[195] Christopher Zara, "Hack Marriage Activists Deface Dictionaries For Marriage Equality, Highlighting a Murky Issue For Post-DOMA Lexicologists," July 17, 2013, IB Times, www.ibtimes.com
[196] Zara, 2013.

CHAPTER 10: SINS OF OMISSION

[197] Henry Chu and Devorah Lauter, "France's same sex marriage law exposes a deep social divide," July 15, 2013, *Los Angeles Times*, www.articles.latimes.com
[198] Chu and Lauter, 2013.
[199] Scott Sayare, "French Protest as Gay Marriage Bill Nears Passage," March 24, 2013, *The New York Times*, www.nytimes.com
[200] Heather Clark, "Battle Continues in Puerto Rico After 200,000 March Against Homosexual 'Marriage' on Island," March 2, 2013, Christian News Network, www.christiannews.net
[201] Andres Schipani, "Colombia votes down gay marriage," April 25, 2013, *The Financial Times*, www.ft.com
[202] James Pach, "Tony Abbott Defeats Kevin Rudd in Australia Election," Sept. 8, 2013, *The Diplomat*, www.thediplomat.com
[203] Brian Brown, "Australia Votes to Reject Rudd and His Promise of Same-Sex Marriage," Sept. 9, 2013, National Organization for Marriage, www.nomblog.com
[204] Monique Garcia, "Illinois gay marriage bill won't pass House this session," May 31, 2013, *Chicago Tribune*, www.chicagotribune.com
[205] Leon Stafford, "Chick-fil-A keeps growing despite uproar," Jan. 29, 2013, *Atlanta Journal-Constitution*, www.ajc.com
[206] Doug Mainwaring, "I'm gay and I oppose same-sex marriage," March 8, 2013, *The Public Discourse*, www.thepublicdiscourse.com
[207] Mainwaring, March 2013.
[208] Mainwaring, March 2013.
[209] Mainwaring, March 2013.
[210] Mainwaring, March 2013.

[211] Stephanie Slifer, "Kaitlyn Hunt Update: Charges against girl, 18, in same-sex underage relationship won't be dropped, despite public outcry, Fla. State attorney says," May 21, 2013, CBS News, www.cbsnews.com

[212] Kim Segal and Greg Botelho, "Gay Florida teen Kaitlyn Hunt sent back to jail over explicit texts, images," Aug. 21, 2013, CNN, www.cnn.com

[213] Kim Segal and Greg Botelho, 2013.

[214] Kim Segal and Greg Botelho, 2013.

[215] Robert Muirhead, "New Sex Abuse Warrant for Glastonbury Couple Denied," Sept. 9, 2013, *Glastonbury Patch*, www.glastonbury.patch.com

[216] Muirhead, 2013.

CHAPTER 11: PLAYING THE NUMBERS GAME

[217] Caitlin Stark, 2013.

[218] Regnerus, 2012.

[219] "Gay Couples in Red-State America Consider Bluer Pastures," Drew Katchen, April 14, 2013, MSNBC, www.msnbc.com

[220] Mainwaring, April 2013.

[221] Mainwaring, April 2013.

[222] Durso, L.E. and Gates, G. J., "Serving Our Youth: Findings From a National Survey of Services Providers Working with Lesbian, Gay, Bisexual and Transgender Youth Who Are Homeless or At Risk of Becoming Homeless," 2012, The Williams Institute with True Colors Fund and The Palette Fund.

[223] Josh Sanburn, "A Midwestern Mayor Evangelizes for Gay Marriage – and Its Economic Bonanza," Sept. 9, 2013, *Time*, www.time.com

[224] Richard D. Mohr, "Gay marriage would bring money to Illinois," Aug. 2, 2013, *Chicago Tribune*, www.chicagotribune.com

[225] Sarah Jean Seman, "Illinois Needs Money, Legalize Gay Marriage," Sept. 23, 2013, Townhall, www.townhall.com

[226] Angeliki Kastanis, M.V. Lee Badgett, "Estimating the Economic Boost of Marriage Equality in Delaware," May 2013, Williams Institute, www.williamsinstitute.law.ucla.edu

[227] Melanie Hicken, "Average wedding bill in 2012: $28,400," March 10, 2013, CNN, www.money.cnn.com

CHAPTER 12: WE ONLY REPORT THE POLLS RESULTS THAT WE LIKE...

[228] Gary Langer, "Poll Tracks Dramatic Rise In Support for Gay Marriage," Mar. 18, 2013, ABC News, www.abcnews.go.com

[229] "85% Think Christian Photographer has Right to Turn Down Same-Sex Wedding Job," July 12, 2013, Rasmussen Reports, www.rasmussenreports.com

[230] Jonathan Oosting, "Poll: Michigan voters wary of gay marriage legislation, ballot measure," Aug. 6, 2013, www.blog.mlive.com

[231] Markus Schmidt, "New poll finds majority of Virginians support same-sex marriage," July 11, 2013, *Richmond Times-Dispatch*, www.timesdispatch.com

[232] Schmidt, 2013.

[233] Andrew Walker and Ryan Anderson, "Refusing to Stay Silent: A Millennial Case for Marriage," May 21, 2013, *Citizen Magazine*, www.citizenlink.com

[234] Tom Heneghan, "French gay marriage opponents stage march," May 26, 2013, Reuters, www.reuters.com

CHAPTER 13: HELP FROM HOLLYWOOD

[235] "Meet the Press," March 31, 2013, NBC, http://www.youtube.com/watch?v=Mvqtd26Zkvk

[236] *Holy Bible*, King James Version, Numbers 13:33

[237] *Holy Bible*, KJV, Numbers 13:33

[238] "MPAA Ratings," Filmbug, www.filmbug.com

[239] "About the TV Ratings and V-Chip," The TV Parental Guidelines, www.tvguidelines.org

[240] Listing for "The Real World," Wikipedia, www.wikipedia.org

[241] "NBC Canceled Show Displaying Gay Marriage as 'The New Normal,'" May 14, 2013, *Christian Post*, www.crossmap.christianpost.com

[242] Shapiro, 2013.

[243] GLAAD website, www.glaad.org (Accessed Sept. 19, 2013)

[244] Mainwaring, March 2013.

[245] Wikipedia listing for "Noah's Arc," Accessed Sept. 20, 2013, www.wikipedia.org

[246] Paul Strand, "Covert Agenda: U.S. Didn't Become Pro-Gay Overnight," June 28, 2013, *Charisma News*, www.charismanews.com

CHAPTER 15: WHAT COMES NEXT?

[247] Ellen Sturtz, "Why I confronted the first lady," June 7, 2013, *The Washington Post*, www.washingtonpost.com

[248] Dave Montez and Wilson Cruz, "The Culture War Isn't Remotely Over," May 2013, *The Atlantic*, www.theatlantic.com